Match of My Life

SUNDERLAND

KNOW THE SCORE BOOKS PUBLICATIONS

CULT HEROES	Author	ISBN
CHELSEA	Leo Moynihan	1-905449-00-3
NEWCASTLE	Dylan Younger	1-905449-03-8
SOUTHAMPTON	Jeremy Wilson	1-905449-01-1
WEST BROM	Simon Wright	1-905449-02-X

MATCH OF MY LIFE	Editor	ISBN
ENGLAND WORLD CUP	Massarella & Moynihan	1-905449-52-6
EUROPEAN CUP FINALS	Ben Lyttleton	1-905449-57-7
FA CUP FINALS (1953-1969)	David Saffer	1-905449-53-4
FULHAM	Michael Heatley	1-905449-51-8
LEEDS	David Saffer	1-905449-54-2
LIVERPOOL	Leo Moynihan	1-905449-50-X
SHEFFIELD UNITED	Nick Johnson	1-905449-62-3
STOKE CITY	Simon Lowe	1-905449-55-0
SUNDERLAND	Rob Mason	1-905449-60-7
SPURS	Allen & Massarella	1-905449-58-5
WOLVES	Simon Lowe	1-905449-56-9

HARRY HARRIS	Author	ISBN
WORLD CUP DIARY	Harry Harris	1-905449-90-9
HOLD THE BACK PAGE	Harry Harris	1-905449-91-7

AUTOBIOGRAPHY	Author	ISBN
TACKLES LIKE A FERRET (England Cover)	Paul Parker	1-905449-47-X
TACKLES LIKE A FERRET (Manchester United Cover)	Paul Parker	1-905449-46-1

FOOTBALL FICTION	Author	ISBN
BURKSEY The Autobiography of a Football God	Peter Morfoot	1-905449-49-6

CRICKET	Author	ISBN
MOML: THE ASHES	Pilger & Wightman	1-905449-63-1

FORTHCOMING PUBLICATIONS IN 2007

CULT HEROES	Author	ISBN
CELTIC	David Potter	978-1-905449-08-8
DERBY	David McVay	978-1-905449-06-4
MANCHESTER CITY	David Clayton	978-1-905449-05-7
RANGERS	Paul Smith	978-1-905449-07-1

MATCH OF MY LIFE	Editor	ISBN
BOLTON WANDERERS	David Saffer	978-1-905449-64-4
FA CUP FINALS (1970-1989)	David Saffer	978-1-905449-65-1
HULL	Grahame Lloyd	978-1-905449-66-8
MANCHESTER UNITED	Sam Pilger	978-1-905449-59-0

GENERAL FOOTBALL	Author	ISBN
OUTCASTS The Lands FIFA Forgot	Steve Menary	978-1-905449-31-6
PARISH TO PLANET A History of Football	Dr Eric Midwinter	978-1-905449-30-9
MY PREMIERSHIP DIARY Reading's Season in the Premiership	Marcus Hahnemann	978-1-905449-33-0

PUB BORE: 1001 incredible facts to bore your mates with	ISBN
MANCHESTER UNITED	978-1-905449-80-4
NEWCASTLE UNITED	978-1-905449-81-1
SUNDERLAND	978-1-905449-82-8

CRICKET	Author	ISBN
THE 2006/7 ASHES IN PICTURES	Andrew Searle	978-1-905449-44-6
GROVEL! The 1976 West IndiesTour of England	David Tossell	978-1-905449-43-9
MY AUTOBIOGRAPHY	Shaun Udal	978-1-905449-42-2
SMILE LIKE U MEAN IT	Paul Smith	978-1-905449-45-3

Match of My Life

SUNDERLAND

Editor: Rob Mason

Series Editor: Simon Lowe
Know The Score Books Limited

www.knowthescorebooks.com

First published in the United Kingdom
by Know The Score Books Limited, 2006

Know The Score Books Limited
118 Alcester Road
Studley
Warwickshire
B80 7NT

www.knowthescorebooks.com

A CIP catalogue record is available for this book from the British Library
ISBN-10: 1-905449-60-7   ISBN-13: 978-1-905449-60-6

Jacket and book design by Lisa David

Printed and bound in Great Britain
By Cromwell Press, Trowbridge, Wiltshire

Editor's Acknowledgements

Thanks to Tania Henzell and Gillian Scott at SAFC for their help with transcribing interviews, Martin Walker at SAFC for his help in obtaining photographs and my fellow Sunderland AFC historian Mike Gibson for his valuable comments. Thanks also to: Everton historian Tony Onslow, Peter Rogers of Norwich City, Andy Exley at Arsenal and Dick Mattrick of Swindon Town.

A sincere thank you is also due to all of the former Sunderland players featured in this book. Their time and co-operation was willingly given in every case and time after time the lifelong bond they feel with Sunderland supporters was always to the fore.

Rob Mason
October 2006

Photographs in this book are reproduced by kind permission of:
Sunderland AFC, Len Ashurst, EMPICS

Front cover:
Top left Niall Quinn
Bottom left Jimmy Montgomery's double save in the 1973 FA Cup final
Bottom right Gary Rowell hat-trick

Rear cover:
Top left Kevin Ball lifts the Championship trophy
Top middle Gary Bennett
Top right 1990 Play-off final ticket
Bottom Charlie Hurley

Contents

Introduction

Over the years I've lost count of the number of players and managers at Sunderland who, not long after their arrival, come out with the line that they had never realised how big a club Sunderland is. Some people might not realise it before they come to the north east, but they certainly do once they've arrived on Wearside. Time after time when I interview former Sunderland players, the impact the club and its fans had on them invariably stands out, even if they have played for a whole host of clubs during their careers.

The dozen players invited to contribute to this book all have great tales to tell. Four of the dozen are native to the north east, but without exception they all remain enthralled by the red and whites. Indeed, of the eight from outside of the region six now have their homes in the area, the exceptions being Marco Gabbiadini, who lives not far away in York, and Hertfordshire based 'Player of the Century' Charlie Hurley, a man whose love for Sunderland and its supporters is legendary.

Every player invited to contribute to Sunderland's 'Match of my Life' book agreed to participate without hesitation. Each was pleased to have the opportunity to talk through their time at the club. It can be amazing asking former players to re-live great games. Tony Norman for instance came into my office at the Stadium of Light and I wished I'd had a video camera on him as he moved to catch or punch every assault on his goal he described. Niall Quinn and Kevin Ball were amongst the others who didn't so much talk me through the match of their lives, they virtually re-enacted them. It was like having personal viewings of old Skinner and Baddiel 'Phoenix from the Flames' sketches.

Len Ashurst and his wife Valerie are always incredibly welcoming. No wonder that, when I speak to players of Len's era (and no outfield player has played more games for Sunderland than Len, who also managed the club), that his name crops up more than any when I ask which of their old team-mates do they keep in contact with. Len opened up his personal scrapbooks for this project and the picture gallery includes several cuttings from Len's collection.

Stan Anderson, Charlie Hurley and Nick Sharkey all played alongside Ashurst in the sixties and were also incredibly helpful, Nick Sharkey even proudly displaying the very match ball with which he scored five times in a 7-1 win over Norwich City in the match of his life.

I'd arranged to meet Marco Gabbiadini at his beautiful Bishops Hotel in York and go for lunch. As luck would have it, when I got there, a workman had just descended to do some work at Marco's home, which meant he had to be in situ. So, having been welcomed at the hotel by Marco's wife Deborah, I was given directions to the Gabbiadini's home. It was inconvenient for Marco and I could have come back another day, but he would have none of that and the lengthy interview went ahead despite the perils of the Gabbiadini household coffee maker and occasional trips to help the workman in the loft!

Gary Bennett and Gary Rowell both do a sterling job summarising Sunderland's matches on BBC Radio Newcastle and Magic 1152 respectively. Their interviews were conducted prior to matches at Portsmouth's Fratton Park and Aston Villa's Villa Park, with Jimmy Montgomery reliving his glorious 1973 Cup final moments at the Stadium of Light. Talking to such legendary figures in football stadiums while the stands are empty strangely brings the memories back. It is as if the goals, the passes, the tackles and the saves are still there; as if you've undertaken some form of time travel where, although the pitch might be bereft of bodies, the mind can still see the great moments and hear the roar of bygone crowds.

Roker Park has long since been a housing estate, but take a walk around there even now and it's not hard to almost see Vic Halom's winner against Manchester City in the 1973 FA Cup run or Gordon Armstrong's last minute header to beat Chelsea in the 1992 FA Cup quarter-final replay, to visualise Charlie Hurley being chaired around the pitch by that great team of 1964 or to think of the glory sides of the thirties and earlier that our Dads and Grandads watched.

If you are interested in the history of Sunderland then the gem sparking at the centre of the jewels in this book is the chapter that begins the volume. Well over 800 players have represented Sunderland since its foundation in 1879. None of them has scored as many goals for the club as the 228 local lad Bobby Gurney managed. That's not counting the nine he scored for the reserves in his first match after signing for his home town team! Being joint top scorer in the league with 31 in Sunderland's 1935/36 championship winning season and the scorer of the Lads' first ever goal beneath the twin towers of Wembley in the FA Cup winning year of 1937 gives Gurney a very special place at the club he served from 1925 until 1946.

It was that Wembley goal that gave me reason to visit Bobby at his East Herrington home in 1992. Sunderland had reached the FA Cup Final that year and I wanted to interview Bobby for the FA Cup final programme.

I spent a couple of hours talking to a man whose memory was still vivid. His recollections of that 3-1 win over Bill Shankly's Preston were duly used in the 1992 FA Cup final programme, but the other 95% of that interview has never seen the light of day until now. Bobby passed away in 1994, but with the permission of his family I'm delighted to use the opportunity afforded by this book to share his memories of his early days alongside stars of the twenties like Albert McInroy and Warney Cresswell as well as his recollections of the great games of the thirties, including the game he thought was the greatest he ever played in, a ten goal FA Cup epic at Everton.

Sunderland has had many fantastic eras. From 'The Team of All The Talents' in the 1890s, the Charlie Buchan side that came so close to the 'double' in 1913, Bobby Gurney's league and cup winning team of the thirties, Charlie Hurley's fabulous 1964 side, Stokoe's Stars of 1973 and the record breaking 105 point team that cheered up Peter Reid in 1999. Niall Quinn was the Queen Bee of that side that his team-mates buzzed around. With Niall now drawn back to Sunderland as Chairman, the backing of the Drumaville group and with Roy Keane as manager, there is hope that another great era for the Black Cats is about to unfold. If in a decade or two someone produces a book that is a sequel to this one I'd love to think the players of the future will have stories to tell that are as dramatic and full of spirit as those contained here.

Rob Mason
September 2006

Dedication

This book is dedicated to Bob Mason, (1930-2006), my dad, who first took me to watch the Lads in 1967 and attended the 1973 FA Cup final with me . He passed away aged 75 during the writing of this book, the span of which covers almost all of his life.

Foreword

ROY KEANE

If you are fortunate enough to have a long football career you will play in hundreds of matches. Every one of them is important and in every one you should endeavour to do the very best you can. Of course once you have retired and can reflect upon your playing days some games stand out more than others.

Having played under Brian Clough, I've long since been aware of some of the great days at Sunderland because whenever I came to play in the north east for Nottingham Forest, he would make sure we all knew what it was all about! Since I've been at Sunderland I've seen for myself the deep feeling that people have for the club and reading the stories in this book shows that the players can feel as deeply about the club as the supporters do.

There are many great names in this book, players who gave the club fantastic service, all of them playing many games for Sunderland. Choosing a 'Match of their Life' must have been very difficult, but they have chosen some classic games as well as sharing with us some great stories about the characters of their era.

I played in some tremendous matches at Sunderland during my own playing days and now as manager I'm aiming to be here for some thrilling games in the seasons to come.

Roy Keane
October 2006

BOBBY GURNEY
CENTRE-FORWARD 1925–1946

BORN   13 October 1907, Silksworth, Sunderland. Died 21st April 1994
SIGNED   7 May 1925 from Bishop Auckland
SUNDERLAND CAREER   390 appearances, 228 goals
HONOURS   1 League Championship, 1 FA Cup, 1 full England cap,
1 full England unofficial appearance
LEFT   Retired May 1946

Bobby Gurney is Sunderland's all time leading goalscorer. 31 of his 228 goals for his home town club came in the Championship winning season of 1935/36. A year later Bobby scored Sunderland's first ever goal at Wembley and first ever goal in an FA Cup Final when netting the equaliser as Preston North End were beaten 3-1. Renowned for his never say die attitude and the ability to score 'impossible' goals, Bobby is one of only four players to ever score five goals in a game for Sunderland and scored four goals in a game on three occasions, one of these being on a day Sunderland won 7-2 away to Birmingham to clinch the League Championship.

This previously unpublished interview was conducted in 1992.

Everton 6 v Sunderland 4 (after extra time)

FA Cup Fourth Round replay
Wednesday 30 January 1935

Goodison Park
Attendance 59,213

Gurney takes Goodison's greatest ever game into extra time

Teams

Chosen by Committee	**Managers**	Johnny Cochrane
Ted Sagar	1	Jimmy Thorpe
Billy Cook	2	Bill Murray
Jack Jones	3	Alex Hall
Cliff Britton	4	Charlie Thomson
Tommy Gee	5	Bert Johnston
Jock Thomson	6	Alex Hastings
Albert Geldard	7	Bert Davis
Nat Cunliffe	8	Raich Carter
Dixie Dean	9	Bobby Gurney
Alec Stephenson	10	Patsy Gallacher
Jackie Coulter	11	Jimmy Connor
Coulter 13, 31, 93	**Scorers**	Davis 40, Connor 80, 99
Stephenson 75		Gurney 89
Geldard 111, 119		

Referee: E Pinkston

ONE OF THE most important games I played in for Sunderland was against Everton. It was a Cup replay in 1935. We played Everton four times that season and three of the games produced 25 goals! We were top of the league until Christmas Day when we went to Goodison Park and got well beaten 6-2, but we went back to the top when we hammered Everton 7-0 at Roker Park the following day. It was normal in those days to play on Christmas Day and Boxing Day and it was usual to have two games against the same team at Christmas or Easter.

I had scored three goals in those two games and a week or two later I got a hat-trick against Fulham in the FA Cup Third round and who should we be drawn against in the next round but Everton at Roker Park! It wasn't a very good game, it was a stop-start kind of affair with lots of free-kicks and it finished 1-1.

The replay at Goodison Park was the following Wednesday afternoon. There was a big crowd with plenty of Sunderland supporters there because special trains had been laid on. It turned out to be a great game. It was a game that they raved over for years on Merseyside. Everton beat us 6-4 after extra-time.

There had been some trouble in the first game, so they changed the referee for the replay to a fellow called Eddie Pinkston from Birmingham. The referee was so strict that this time the players just got on with playing football. Goodison Park was a wonderful place because Everton were by far the biggest team in Liverpool in those days, having won the League in 1931/32 and followed that achievement up with an FA Cup victory the following season. They had also boasted the legendary Dixie Dean, who had scored a record 60 goals in the 1927/28 season, as their centre-forward.

I scored the equaliser with an overhead kick in the last couple of minutes of normal time to make it 3-3 and take the match into extra-time.During the extra half--hour, I remember Patsy Gallacher missed a sitter that would have made it 5-4 to us. That was the only time that we would have been in front, but they came at us and got two simple late goals to win an epic game that, as a pure football match, I rate as the best I played in.

I was at Sunderland from 1925 until I retired after the war. I've got memories of going training at Roker Park in 1925. The pitch was always the same as when I first went there, but the surrounds and the stands completely changed. Back in 1925 there was an old wooden stand or grandstand. I can remember going down there to report for training at the beginning of July 1925 and there was just a little, narrow wooden door for players to enter. Billy Williams the trainer would stand outside.

You had to report for training at half past nine and Billy would meet the players coming in. You went through the narrow doorway, turned left down a passage past the visiting team's dressing room on the left and then further down the passage was the home team's dressing room, which was bigger. It included a bath and a slipper bath. There was a treatment table in the middle of the room.

When you came out to play a match at Roker Park in those days, the visitors had to come down the narrow passage towards the home team dressing room and then you went up three wooden steps and finally some steps down and out onto the pitch. The people who stood in the enclosure could turn around and shake hands with the directors. I cannot tell you where the directors went for a cup of tea at half-time, but they certainly had nothing like what they've got now!

The secretary/manager was Bob Kyle, his office was at the bottom of the ground. When you came around the corner of Roker Baths Road around the Roker End and up towards the main entrance, that's where the secretary's office was. It was a big wooden hut. They had a billiards table in there with seats around. The players had to go in there after Thursday afternoon training for when word came through about the team. They usually had a Board meeting to pick the first team and the second team.

The office boy would come in with the team sheet and pin it up so that everyone could see whether they were in the first team or the second team. If the first team were going away for a Saturday game they'd usually meet up at the Central Station on the Friday. The Reserves had to report to Roker Park and if they were away they would get a coach from there.

The old wooden stand ran more or less the length of the pitch. I believe it was pulled down in 1929 as soon as the season finished because they had to get the new one built for the start of the 1929/30 season. It wasn't quite ready when we reported back for training and we had to go to Chiswick's football field next to Redby School to do our training. The old Clock Stand was an old wooden stand. It was smaller than the main stand, but it had seats at the back with standing at the front.

I was in and out of the first team from about 1926 until around 1929/30 when Davie Halliday, the first team centre-forward, was transferred to Arsenal and I came into the team.

Before that, though, my first competitive game at Roker Park was against Hartlepools United reserves. We won 14-0 and I scored nine goals. It used to cost about sixpence to watch the reserves and you got a lot of people coming to watch us because we had a good side. If I remember rightly between 1925 to1928 we won the North East League three years in succession. I remember a midweek reserve game at Roker Park where we won 9-1 and our outside-left Billy Death scored seven. I can remember him cutting in from the wing at the Roker End, running along the byeline and hitting a ferocious shot which the goalkeeper jumped out of the road of as it might have hurt him. He really had a ferocious shot!

In those days you always played a practise game between the reserves and the first team at Roker Park a week or two before the start of the season. I always remember playing for the reserves and leading the first team 4-1! We got stuck into them, but eventually they beat us 5-4.

Davie Halliday was signed about a fortnight before me. I got into the first team as inside-left towards the back end of the 1925/26 season. My first game was against West Ham in London. We lost 3-2, but I played alongside Davie Halliday and scored my first league goal.

My home debut was against Arsenal. It was the first time Charlie Buchan had been back to Sunderland since his transfer. I believe Charlie Parker was our centre-half that day. That was the first time Charlie Buchan was booed at Roker Park because he fouled Charlie. I scored the two goals and we won 2-1. Davie Halliday and the Arsenal goalkeeper were ordered off and it was very rare to get sent off back then.

I played in the FA Cup Final at Wembley when we beat Preston 3-1 in 1937, but I can't say that was the best game I ever played in. It was the most important though, along with the day in 1936 when we clinched the League title with a fantastic win against Birmingham.

One of the big occasions I played in was the day Sunderland had their record home attendance for an FA Cup tie against Derby. I'd learned a bit of a lesson in the first game, which finished 4-4 at the Baseball Ground. We were winning 4-3 with a few seconds remaining when a ball was played up to me. There was only me up at the centre line. In those days the centre forward always stayed up. Their right-back was Tommy Cooper, an England international who later went to Arsenal. There was only a few minutes to go and I always remember saying to myself, "shall I hold it or try and beat him?" What I did, though, was to kick it as far as I could towards the corner flag. That was my mistake because nearly all of their players were nearer our goal and there was a big clearance which came to Dally Duncan, their left-winger, who beat Bill Murray and put a hard ball over from which they equalised. That really stands out in my memory because I knew I should have held the ball.

When we had the replay the following Wednesday, we had stayed at the Roker Hotel and as we walked along to Roker Park it was choc-a-bloc. There was over 75,000 there, hoping to see another goal-packed game, to make it Roker Park's record attendance and it was estimated there were several thousand more who couldn't get in. The ground was packed and spectators were up to the touchline. Whenever there was a corner kick and the taker wanted to get onto the cinder track to take a few steps to kick the ball he had to try and get the crowd to make way for him.

I remember chasing a through ball in the first half with their centre-half Jack Barker. He was just slightly behind me and, as it happened, I just stood on the ball and a fraction of a second later he hit me. I was travelling fast and as I fell I instinctively put my arm out to break my fall, but, in doing so, I damaged my shoulder. I had my arm put in a sling and as there were no substitutes in those days I went on to play on the right wing with the winger replacing me as centre-forward. The match went to extra time, but Derby got a simple goal and beat us one to nothing.

There are several games that really stand out for me. In the Championship year of 1936 at Easter time I remember we needed four points to win the League. There were only two points for a win then and we beat Birmingham 2-1 at Roker Park on Good Friday and then travelled straight to the railway station to travel to Bolton for a game the following day. A win would net us the title, but we got beat 2-1.

We travelled to Birmingham to play the return game on Easter Monday and we beat them 7-2. I scored four of the goals and I probably could have scored another two or three. The forward line was Davis, Carter, myself, Hornby who played instead of Gallacher, and Jimmy Connor was on the left-wing. To a certain extent it was a wonderful game of football from a Sunderland point of view. It was very one-sided, but it gave us players great satisfaction because we clinched the league. We stayed in the New Street Station that night celebrating. We lost games after that, but we knew nobody could catch us.

The 7-2 championship winning game with Birmingham was a great day and capped a wonderful achievement, but there was only one team in the game. In the Everton cup tie there were definitely two teams in it and it was a great match. Both teams played well and there were ten goals scored through good football.

We finished runners up in the league to Arsenal that year. We beat them at home and drew away in front of Highbury's record attendance. Arsenal won the League Championship three years in succession, mainly due to the influence of their legendary manager Herbert Chapman, although George Allinson was in charge for their third title season, 1934/35. They'd won the FA Cup and the Charity Shield as well in the 1930s. In 1935 Arsenal had a Championship dinner and as the runners-up we were invited down as we were on our way to Spain to play three post-season friendlies

The next season, 1935/36, we took the Championship off them. We had a great game with them at Roker Park where we beat them 5-4. We were beating them 4-1 at half-time, they came back to 4-3 and then we got another one to go 5-3 up before they came back to 5-4. In the November of 1936 we took the Charity Shield off them as well and then in 1937 we won the English Cup!

When we won the Championship we scored 109 goals, but the defence let in about eighty. We used to play hell with them! We used to say, "What's the use of us scoring goals if you lot are letting them in?" but they'd just say, "You'll have to make up for it." Raich Carter and I scored over 60 between us and Patsy Gallacher got nineteen. Raich and Patsy were great inside-forwards. Patsy was a very good worker off the ball and was two-footed. Raich was also very good with both feet and with his body swerve, which left defenders for dead.

Sometimes I read in the papers about someone scoring something like his seventh goal of the season in November and I'll think, "We used to score that many in one game!" Not quite, but I once scored five in a game against Liverpool and another time we went to Anfield one Easter Saturday and beat them 6-0, I scored four of them that day. I should've scored five again, but I slid in for one cross and put it over the bar. I still don't know how I didn't score.

I developed this reputation for scoring some 'impossible' goals. My equaliser in the 1937 FA Cup semi-final went through six players. I shoved a ball to Carter and ran for a return and when it came to me I just hit it and it went in. You always need a bit of luck. Sometimes people said I missed the easy ones and scored the impossible ones. The goal I scored in the Cup Final was a freak. We got a corner. I always used to go and stand in front of the goal-keeper to stop him getting a good view of the corner kick. Eddie Burbanks hit this corner towards the penalty spot where all the players were. The Preston goalkeeper was Micky Burns, who used to play for Newcastle. I moved out towards the ball. How Raich Carter got above everyone to head the ball on I don't know, but it came straight to me. Billy Tremelling, their centre-half, should have been covering me, but he was in amongst the players challenging for the ball, so I managed to divert it. All Micky Burns had to do was react, he was two yards off the line and I was on the six yard line. George Harrison was commentating and he said I was offside, but Andy Beattie was full-back for Preston and he played me on. Really all I did was deflect Carter's header.

As well as winning the League Championship, the FA Cup and the Charity Shield with Sunderland, I had the pleasure of playing for England. It all came about because I played for 'The Rest' against England at Roker Park in 1934. Raich Carter was picked for 'The Rest' and I was reserve. George Camsell of Middlesbrough was picked for the England team and a fellow called Milson of Bolton Wanderers was selected for 'The Rest'. Camsell had to cry off injured, so Milson moved into the England team and, as reserve, I came into 'The Rest' team. Our forward line that day was Stanley Matthews, Raich Carter, myself, Ray Westwood of Bolton Wanderers and Eric Bribb of Manchester City. We beat the England team 7-1. Raich Carter scored four goals, I scored two and Eric Bribb scored the other one. It was through that game that Raich Carter was selected to play for England.

Newcastle United's wing-half Sammy Weaver was on our side and he said to me, "You should be selected," but I wasn't. The next year, though, in April 1935, I was selected and Raich Carter was reserve for an England game against Scotland at Hampden Park. I went down to Roker Park on the Monday – which was pay day – when word came through that I'd been selected to play for England the following Saturday. I got my instructions through the post on a card, which had printed on it the time I had to report on the Friday night at a certain hotel in Troon and what you had to bring with you, which was boots and shinpads. You got your shirt, pants and stockings given to you. Scotland had some very good players in those days, though, like Hughie Gallacher and Dally Duncan and we lost 2-0.

A lot of people think I only played for England once, but I actually played twice because I played in that full international where you got a cap and I played against Scotland at Hampden Park in the week before the season started in what was called the King George's Jubilee Trust Fund Game. All the gate money went to King George's charity and instead of getting a cap we got a silver Scottish Loving Cup. The papers still say I only played once for England, but I maintain I played twice. The first game they beat us 2-0 and in the King George game we lost 4-2, but I had the pleasure of scoring one of England's two goals with a header.

I had missed out on an international cap when I played for a schoolboy team. Back then you could leave school the day after you were fourteen. My 14th birthday was in October and I was in the running for a schoolboy international cap. I'd had to go to York for a schoolboy trial match. My father always travelled with me. They only played me in the second half and we heard afterwards that the selectors had gone away at half-time to pick the team and they never saw me play. My father had paid his own expenses and, having a bit of a fiery temper at times, he withdrew me from school as I was over fourteen.

I went to work at the local colliery as the family needed the money. Shortly afterwards word came through from the schoolboy associations that I had been picked, after all, to play for England schoolboys at Newcastle United's ground, but by then I'd left, so I couldn't represent the schoolboy team.

I played for Hetton Juniors. We had a great winger called Sammy Gibbon who was a County cricketer and a good footballer. Somebody wrote in the paper about me. I was scoring a lot of goals at the time, thirteen in one match was my best against Fence Houses YMCA. From that the famous amateur club Bishop Auckland signed me. My ambition was to get out of the pit and become a full-time professional footballer and I worked very hard to achieve it.

I was playing so much for Bishop Auckland and Hetton Juniors that I only got to Roker Park to watch Sunderland on odd days that were few and far between. I always used to go in the Fulwell End with my father because in those days a lot of supporters had their own spots in the ground. I always remember one day in my early schooldays that I was in the wooden stand against a barrier and a crush fell forward and broke the posts of the barrier. Fortunately I wasn't hurt, but that was the sort of thing that happened.

I went straight into Bishop Auckland's first team at sixteen. There were six full amateur internationals in the team. All grown men. I never won the Amateur Cup with Bishop Auckland, but they were a wonderful team. I scored about 17 goals in the season for Bishop Auckland, but I missed quite a bit of it through a neck injury I picked up playing against an amateur team from Sheffield. They wanted me to stay for another season, but something else came up instead.

Whilst I was playing for Bishops there were two workmen electrocuted at Eppleton Colliery. There was a benefit match for widows and orphans between Bishop Auckland and a select team from Sunderland, Newcastle United and Middlesbrough. The outside-left for the select team was old Stan Seymour, who was finishing his career. I scored two goals and I must have played well because Sunderland's old chief scout Bob Wood saw me.

My father would never let me sign for Sunderland until he got a promise from them that they'd look after me. I was only young and some days the trainer at Sunderland, Billy Williams, would let me have a day off when the other players were training. I was only slim and about ten stone then and I didn't need the amount of training some of the older players needed.

I had a good career at the club, but I broke my leg twice. The first time was in the week before my 20th birthday playing for the reserves against Workington. I was chasing a through ball in the first minute. The goalkeeper came out and we collided. I didn't feel anything at first, but after a few seconds the pain came. Fortunately it was only a simple fracture. It was the fibula that was broken. I got carried off into the Workington dressing room and laid on a wooden table. The local doctor looked at me and said it was a severe bruise, but I told him it wasn't. I wasn't taken to hospital.

We always travelled in a special railway coach to matches at Carlisle and Workington. I had no crutches and was only bandaged, so they had to carry me back to the train. We had to change trains at Newcastle and at the station they put me on a little bogey that rattled along the station. When we got back to Sunderland I had to get a taxi to take me to where I lived at Silksworth. The injury was reported to the club doctor, who lived along Stockton Road and he came up to see me on the Sunday. I had it X-Rayed and I ended up in a nursing home near Christ Church. I was in there for about four or five weeks with my leg in a plaster cast, although I was allowed to go home on crutches. I always remember, though, that I had to spend my 20th birthday in the nursing home.

I played my first game back early in January for the Reserves at Scotswood and I got into trouble from the trainer and the assistant manager for running about too much. They said, "you've just recovered from a broken leg". I was quite fit, though, and I was alright.

The second time I broke it was in an FA Cup Fifth Round second replay against Blackburn Rovers at Sheffield Wednesday's ground. I never played again after that. I went through for a through ball, stretched my foot out to push the ball past the goalkeeper, who was Billy Barrow, and I turned my ankle. It caused a hairline crack, so it wasn't as bad as the other one, but I got carried off. The club doctor was there and he couldn't find anything, so it got bandaged up by the trainer.

The manager Johnny Cochrane came in to the dressing room. Johnny at that time was on his last legs at Roker Park and I thought, "well, he's the manager and the team have an important cup game on." He was talking to me about going back on and scoring the winning goal to be the hero. He went to have a wash and when he did I tried to stand up, but as soon as I put my foot down there was terrific pain and I couldn't do it. If I remember rightly we lost to a goal from a corner a couple of minutes from the end of extra-time.

They whipped me back to Monkwearmouth Hospital where they X-Rayed it and saw the crack of a hairline fracture. They didn't bother to put it in a plaster cast because the bandaging was firmly fixed. I was in hospital for about four weeks. While I was in there I was one of the first people to know that Johnny Cochrane had been sacked. He came in on the Thursday morning to see me and told me.

I was the only player in the Cup winning team that he hadn't signed. When he first came, he tried to get rid of all the players who were Bob Kyle's. To him I was a Bob Kyle player. Johnny had come to Roker Park in 1928 after the last match of the season against Middlesbrough, when Boro only had to draw and Sunderland had to win to avoid relegation. I was down to play inside-left. It was the season when I'd first broken my leg, but I'd come back. We were taken away for a week's special training at Saltburn before the match. The trainer Billy Williams took me down onto the beach to try me out. It was such an important game and I was still a youngster really and I was 100% keen to play, but he wouldn't report that I was fit, so that day Sunderland played two outside-lefts, Billy Death and Len Hargreaves. Billy Death played inside-left and it turned out to be his last ever game for Sunderland. George Robinson played his first game that day at outside-right and Sunderland won three nothing. I remember Davie Halliday scored.

I was never ordered off and I only got reported once. We were playing Middlesbrough and we lost 6-0, Carter and Davis were sent off. Hastings, Johnson and I got reported. We were down to nine men and I chased a ball out to the right wing, we had no right-winger as he'd been dismissed, so I raced over and tried to hook a ball over my head to try and keep it in play.

I didn't mean to harm anybody, but with all the trouble just before that the referee thought I'd deliberately kicked the ball into the stand. I had to go to a committee meeting at Darlington. I told them I didn't do it deliberately and I got let off, so I have a clear record, although I can understand the referee's point of view.

We used to train a lot by running on the beach. Billy Dunlop the assistant trainer, would take us for a brisk walk from Roker Park down to the sea front and along to Whitburn cricket ground. When I was a boy we had some of the old stagers in with us, people like Albert McInroy, Warney Cresswell, Arthur Andrews and Ernie England. They'd fall behind and catch a tram up to Whitburn without Billy Dunlop seeing them. They were the crafty ones, the experienced ones. I was nicknamed 'Boy Gurney' and they were men to me, some of them were married and I was the youngest then, but I stayed at Sunderland for a long time and after the war I worked on the coaching staff.

We used to have lots of high scoring matches when I played, but the match against Everton was a great game because of the quality of the football – as well as the fact that there were ten goals. Everton kept the same team as in the first game, but we had brought in Alex Hall instead of Harold Shaw at left-back. If anything, we made the better starts. Jimmy Connor was a wonderful left winger and he put over a couple of great early crosses, but, just as we looked like getting on top, their left winger Jackie Coulter hooked in a shot that beat Jimmy Thorpe in our goal.

A few minutes later I thought I'd equalised with a header, but Ted Sagar pulled off a reaction save that pushed the ball out for a corner. Although the match ended up with ten goals, both goalkeepers actually made some great saves on the day. They had to, it was such a fast open game with both teams playing well that there were goalmouth incidents from start to finish.

We pushed hard for an equaliser, I remember Jimmy Connor hitting the bar, I got to the rebound first, but could only throw myself at it and knock it forward off my chest and Ted Sagar just got to it on the line. We were putting Everton under heavy pressure, but we got hit on the break when Coulter made it 2-0.

Being two goals behind wasn't the sort of thing to put us off. We'd come back from two goals down before, but when Raich Carter had a shot cleared off the line we were starting to think it wasn't going to be our day. But then, just before half-time, Bert Davis managed to score for us and at the break we were sure we could go on and win.

We pushed hard for an equaliser in the second half, I got sent clear and went round the goalkeeper once, only for their left-back Jack Jones (who signed for Sunderland after the war) to race back and clear. Then we should have had a penalty when their centre-half Tommy Gee handballed in the penalty box, but the referee didn't see it. We'd had nearly all of the play in the second half, although to give credit to Everton they had defended well. But then, with just about quarter of an hour left, they made it 3-1 when Alex Stephenson scored, again on the break.

Whenever that happens you have to get a goal back straight away and we did that when Jimmy Connor scored after playing a one-two with me. It's amazing to think that the master of centre-forwards Dixie Dean didn't score in a game where there were ten goals, but he would have done if Jimmy Thorpe hadn't made a wonderful save from him in the last few minutes.

There were only a couple of minutes left when we managed to get the equaliser we deserved. As I said, I used to score all sorts of goals that people often said were 'impossible' goals. I scored from some very narrow angles and with unorthodox shots and this one was an overhead kick that must have caught Ted Sagar by surprise to make it 3-3. He was rooted to the spot.

There were four more goals in extra-time, but sadly from our point of view three of them were for Everton. Jackie Coulter completed his hat-trick pretty much straight after extra-time got started, so having been behind in the game for so long we were behind again just after getting back to all square. Jimmy Connor made it 4-4 with a first time shot, but Everton's right winger Albert Geldard scored twice late on to make it 6-4 in a game where eight of the goals had been scored by wingers and not one had been a header.

Obviously it's nicer to think of games that we won and we won some important games when I was at Sunderland, but as a game of football that match at Everton would take some beating.

STAN ANDERSON
RIGHT-HALF 1949–1963

BORN   27 February 1934, Horden, County Durham
SIGNED   June 1949 as Amateur, professional February 1951
SUNDERLAND CAREER   447 games, 35 goals
HONOURS   2 England caps, 1 England B cap, 4 England Under 23 caps,
3 England schoolboy caps, 1 Division Two championship
LEFT   Transferred to Newcastle United, November 1963; £30,000

Only Len Ashurst can equal Stan Anderson's claim to have played over 400
league games for Sunderland as an outfield player. A classy wing-half, Stan was
the only Sunderland player to earn a full England cap during the sixties. Being
sent off when representing England Under 23s in 1957 is thought to have
seriously damaged his international career, but in the north east his stature in
the game is exceptional. A rare home grown player in Sunderland's 'Bank of
England' fifties side, Stan was the last of that team to leave, doing so in contro-
versial circumstances when Alan Brown bombed him out to Newcastle with
whom Stan won promotion. He later managed AEK Athens, Doncaster and
Bolton in addition to spells as assistant manager at Manchester City and QPR.

Sunderland 2 v Arsenal 1

FA Cup Third Round
Saturday 7 January 1961

Roker Park
Attendance 58,575

Two goals from Stan cap an outstanding personal performance as Sunderland beat a top flight side for the first time since their first ever relegation in 1958

Teams

Alan Brown	**Managers**	George Swindin
Peter Wakeham	1	Jack Kelsey
Colin Nelson	2	Eddie MacGill
Len Ashurst	3	Billy McCullough
Stan Anderson	4	Terry Neill
Charlie Hurley	5	Mel Charles
Jim McNab	6	Vic Groves
Harry Hooper	7	John Barnwell
Ambrose Fogarty	8	David Herd
Ian Lawther	9	Geoff Strong
Willie McPheat	10	George Eastham
Jackie Overfield	11	Jackie Henderson
Anderson 51, 77	**Scorers**	Herd 6

Referee: A Ellis

I PLAYED NEARLY 450 games for Sunderland, but sometimes I get the impression that people think I just played one, against Arsenal in the Cup when I scored twice. It's the game everybody always asks me about whenever I visit Sunderland. It was by no means the only decent game I ever played, but it has a great significance in Sunderland.

Until 1958 Sunderland was the only team in the country who had only ever played in the top flight. But by the time of this game Arsenal were doing well in the First Division and, for the now Second Division Sunderland to beat them, gave the supporters a taste of being back in the big time. It brought a touch of glory back to Wearside. Sunderland supporters had been used to it over the years, but hadn't had a taste for a while. Beating Arsenal showed that the club could get back to the top where it should be.

For a lot of the players it was a first taste of a really big game. We had lads in the side who had barely played in the First Division or, for many, not at all. After this match people like Len Ashurst and Jimmy McNab knew what playing a really big game was all about and what was needed to achieve a victory in such a match.

I'd played in big games throughout the fifties when we were a side full of big names that everyone liked to try and beat, but to play against a team like Arsenal in front of a huge crowd and then outplay them and fully deserve to win made it a game that still lives in the memory of people who were there and it set us off on a great cup run.

The crowd at Sunderland was unbelievably noisy. The Roker Roar was fantastic. The noise would crescendo as attacks built up and the noise would echo around the ground so much that Roker Park would reverberate. One end would try and outdo the other and you'd end up with a huge roar.

In the two seasons since we'd been relegated we'd struggled in the lower half of mid-table as Alan Brown built a young side. But when the Arsenal game came around we were on a twelve match unbeaten run and were flying. We'd beaten Luton 7-1 a week earlier and, although we finished well short of promotion, in the end we reached sixth place and started to look like we could mount a serious promotion challenge which we did in the years that followed. Had we not got involved in a long cup run who knows how close we might have got in 1961.

That run to the FA Cup quarter-final could have been nipped in the bud by the Gunners. Arsenal had some terrific players such as George Eastham, Mel Charles and David Herd and in the first half hour they were comfortably the better team. Peter Wakeham made a couple of excellent saves in our goal, but we couldn't argue that they didn't deserve to take the lead when David Herd put them 1-0 up, although it was a very unfortunate goal from our point of view when it came.

Having been on that twelve match unbeaten run we had belief in ourselves and as we got to grips with Arsenal we felt that if we could get an equaliser we were capable of going on to beat them.

I didn't score many headers during my career, but early on in the second half I managed to meet a corner-kick and beat Jack Kelsey with a plain and simple header. There was nothing spectacular about it, it was just a routine cross and header, but it was an important goal. Sometimes goals are measured by their quality – a long range strike or a dribble round a few defenders, but on this occasion this goal was great because it reinforced that belief that we could beat this team.

I had a good understanding with Harry Hooper, who was on the right wing, and Amby Fogarty who was playing inside him. The three of us were linking up well and causing Arsenal plenty of problems and when the winning goal came it was Harry Hooper who put me through. I always rated Harry very highly. He was a very clever player. If you were ever in trouble you could just give him the ball because he had the knack of being able to beat people at very close quarters.

Against Arsenal, when he got the ball on the move he was just inside the Gunners' half. Amby Fogarty made a run up the touchline to take a defender away and I made a twenty five yard run into space. I couldn't believe it because there was no-one there with me as the gap opened up and Harry gave me the ball just where I wanted it. Jack Kelsey came about eight yards off his line to try and narrow the angle. I remember deciding not to try and beat him at his near post, but to go across him and shoot for the far side of goal and it was a great feeling when the ball just scraped in! There was such a lot of joy around Roker and when the final whistle sounded the scenes were terrific. We had a team capable of beating Arsenal and, after the worst period in the club's history with the fall out from relegation, Sunderland were at long last on the way back.

We were drawn away to Liverpool in the Fourth Round. Like us they were a Second Division side at the time. We'd already been to Anfield and drawn in the league and we went there and won 2-0 with a goal apiece from Harry Hooper and Ian Lawther, our Northern Irish centre-forward, who scored more than twice as many goals as anyone else that season.

Having got past Liverpool we were given another awkward away tie, this time at Norwich. Liverpool and Norwich finished the season third and fourth in the Second Division with us sixth. Although the Fifth Round trip to Carrow Road came in February, we hadn't yet played them in the league. The Norwich tie was in my opinion the best team performance that side ever produced. The game stands out possibly even more than the Arsenal game because it was about the whole team rather than some individuals doing particularly well.

Norwich really put us under the cosh and we had to defend and really battle for probably eighty minutes of the game. Everyone really had to give everything to keep us level and then, from one of our few attacks, we got a corner from which Charlie Hurley scored with the most magnificent header you will ever see. He met the cross about fifteen yards from goal and gave it such a thwack with perfect timing that it absolutely rocketed into the net. What a goal it was!

We were due a home draw in the quarter-finals after a couple of away ties and we got one. It was a plum draw against Tottenham Hotspur. They would end the season as the first team of the Twentieth Century to achieve the 'double' of First Division Championship and the FA Cup, but we came so close to knocking them out at Roker Park.

Spurs went 1-0 up early on when Cliff Jones scored from a corner, but we'd been 1-0 down at half-time against Arsenal and regardless of the fact we were up against the country's top side with players like Dave Mackay and Danny Blanchflower in their line-up we felt that we had it within us to come from behind in this game as well. We felt this even more when, just as in the Arsenal game, we equalised a few minutes into the second half. We really had them under the cosh then, the Roker Roar was in overdrive and Spurs simply didn't know what was happening to them. At one point I looked at Blanchflower and he'd gone white!

But we couldn't find that vital winning goal. The match ended up 1-1 and we got hammered 5-1 in the replay when Tottenham showed why they were good enough to do the 'double'. I can't help wondering, though, what might have happened if we'd been able to get a winning goal at Roker.

I'd played in a couple of semi-finals earlier in my career at Sunderland, but had come off second best both times. The 1955 semi-final against Manchester City at Villa Park should never have been played. The pitch was waterlogged and before the game we thought it was bound to be postponed. Our manager was Bill Murray who had first come to the club as a player in the twenties. It got to the point where, before the game, he thought it would be called off and when the referee decided to try and make a start we all thought it was simply because so many Sunderland supporters had travelled such a long way in difficult conditions – remember there were no motorways then – and that at least there would be a bit of football for them.

We were all looking around at each other thinking, "This is ridiculous." It was an absolute quagmire and even big George Aitken, on one occasion I remember, only managed to kick the ball two or three yards, so for ball-playing people such as Len Shackleton it was impossible. It had been raining solidly for days. We'd stayed in Buxton for three or four days when the rain simply hadn't let up. Unbelievably the semi-final was never abandoned and we ended up losing 1-0. It was bad enough losing, but to lose in such a manner when football hadn't really been given a chance was even more disappointing. I'd just been married and my wife was in the stands. When I met her afterwards, the coat she was wearing was like a rag it was so soaked through and the supporters making their way home must have needed days to dry out.

Had we won we'd have met Newcastle at Wembley. They beat York in a semi-final replay at Roker Park and went on to win the Cup. We got to the semi-final again a year later, but only after knocking cup holders Newcastle out in the quarter--final on their own patch.

We'd had a disastrous Christmas. On Boxing Day 1955, Newcastle had recorded their greatest ever win against us by hammering us 6-1 at Roker Park. A day later we went to St. James's Park and led 1-0 at half-time, but then we got beat 3-1, so when we were drawn away to Newcastle in the Cup quarter-final they certainly fancied their chances.

We hadn't been doing particularly well in the lead up to the game, but I remember sitting with Shack in the dressing room before the match and he was insisting that we could win because, as he argued, after beating us so convincingly earlier in the season, they'd be thinking all they had to do was turn up. Newcastle weren't helped by the fact that Jimmy Scoular, who was a very influential figure for them, had been struggling with an injury and, just to make sure he was feeling the effects of it, Billy Elliott well and truly clattered him in the first few minutes!

We won the match 2-0. Ray Daniel took care of Jackie Milburn and Bill Holden got both goals. It was a great result, but it wasn't a good game. I always look at displays and how well we played and that wasn't one of the best by any means, but it meant that we turned the tables on them after the league results and made it through to the semi-final again.

Being the underdogs is often an advantage. Shack was right about Newcastle that day and sometimes if you are the favourites you can't help going into a game thinking that you will win whereas underdogs often fight more. A classic case was just a couple of years before that Newcastle game. In the 1954 World Cup Hungary were the world's best side. They'd put six past England at Wembley and seven past England in Hungary in the previous year or two and hammered Germany 8-3 in the tournament itself but when they met Germany again in the Final the Germans beat them 3-2. It was a great shock, but it can happen.

Although they ended up finishing just ahead of us in the league we felt we were the favourites against Birmingham City in the semi-final at Hillsborough. We'd beaten them at their place earlier in the season and in fact went on to do the double over them in the league, but in the semi-final we lost 3-0 and really never got started. That was a huge disappointment.

There were some great characters in that side as there were throughout my time at Sunderland. My favourite was always Len Shackleton. He was such a talented player. It's no use thinking back really, but he'd be worth £40m now. If he could bend the old leather ball the way he used to I can only imagine what he'd do with the balloons they play with now. I see Beckham hit wonderful free-kicks, but there's no effort in it in the same sense there had to be when Shack made the ball do tricks for him.

Ray Daniel was a class player when he turned it on. Billy Elliott, Arthur Hudgell and George Aitken were great characters. In my early days in the first team I even played a couple of matches alongside Johnny Mapson, who had played in the 1937 FA Cup winning team. By then he was a veteran, of course, and a huge figure in the club's history who I really looked up to.

Ken Chisholm was great fun. He used to kid me that he had been the youngest fighter pilot in World War Two. In fact he HAD flown with the RAF, but he kept pulling my leg all the time! Ken could be a bit slow and ponderous as an inside-left, but he was a lovely man. Our South African centre-forward Ted Purdon was really funny as well. I always rated him as a player, but he went off the rails a bit as he liked to join Ken Chisholm for a bit of 'socialising'!

However the man who really looked after me was big Fred Hall. He knew all the best jokes and so many naughty verses I don't know how he remembered them all, but he could keep us entertained all the way from Sunderland to Kings Cross! In one of my early games I was up against Billy Wright, famous of course as the first man to play 100 times for England. He was playing on the left of midfield and early in the game he came right through me and knocked the wind right out of me. Big Fred picked me up and said, "Right Stan, son. Next time he comes towards you, show him inside and let him go past you." A few minutes later I did just that and as Wright went past I didn't see Fred coming, but I heard this awful sound as he dived in two footed and left him in a heap. Wright never seemed to cross the half-way line any more after that!

I'd been in the team for a few years when Sunderland signed Charlie Hurley. Charlie was a fantastic centre-half and was officially captain at the start of the 1958/59 season, which was the one after Sunderland's first ever relegation. As it happened, though, he was injured at the start of the season and he went to Browny [Manager Alan Brown] and said he thought that I should be captain while he was injured. We lost three of the four games Charlie missed, the last of them 6-2 away to Fulham.

When he was fit again I expected him to pick up the ball and lead the team out, but he said, "No, you keep the captaincy," which was nice of him and so I stayed captain until I left five years later, when he took over. I captained every team I played for, so it was great to captain Sunderland.

Playing for the team I supported was always a privilege and a pleasure for me. I never wanted to leave Sunderland, but eventually Browny 'bombed' me out. At one point I couldn't even get a game for the reserves when I was fit. Joe Harvey was desperate for me to sign for Newcastle and I was just as keen not to go. I knew there'd be trouble if I switched stripes and I was from a family of dyed in the wool red and whites. In the end, though, I made the move after playing the first 11 games of Sunderland's 1963/64 promotion season.

I had a Testimonial back at Sunderland at the end of that season as a Newcastle player, which was remarkable, but it all worked out well because the supporters were overjoyed to celebrate Sunderland's promotion and so was I. I may have moved on by then, but I knew I had played my part. That night against Arsenal in 1961 had signalled that Sunderland were on the way back to the big time and after a couple of near misses in '62 and '63 the club were back in the top flight which is where a club of Sunderland's stature should always be.

NICK SHARKEY
STRIKER 1958–1966

BORN   4 May 1943, Helensburgh, Dumbartonshire
SIGNED   May 1958 as Amateur, professional May 1960
SUNDERLAND CAREER   117 games, 62 goals
HONOURS   Promotion from Division Two 1963/64
LEFT   Transferred to Leicester City, October 1966; £15,000

The only man living to have scored five goals in a competitive peacetime game for Sunderland, and one of only four players to ever achieve the feat, Sharkey was a goal-scoring machine. Still a teenager when he scored those five goals, the Scot had once scored thirteen times in a youth team game and managed as many as 187 in one astonishing season at junior levels. Despite averaging better than a goal every two games in well over a hundred appearances for The Lads, Sharkey was transferred following the arrival of the former Scotland manager Ian McColl, who had made it clear he didn't fancy him as a player when Sharkey arrived for training with the Scotland squad which had been called together by a team of selectors.

Sunderland 7 v Norwich City 1

League Division Two
Wednesday 20 March 1963

Roker Park
Attendance 42,393

Teenager Sharkey scores five just five games after replacing injury-stricken goal machine Brian Clough

Teams

Alan Brown	**Managers**	Ron Ashman
Jimmy Montgomery	1	Sandy Kennon
Colin Nelson	2	Phil Kelly
Len Ashurst	3	Barry Staton
Stan Anderson	4	Dick Scott
Charlie Hurley	5	Ron Ashman
Jimmy McNab	6	Joe Mullet
Jimmy Davison	7	Gerry Mannion
George Herd	8	Tommy Bryceland
Nick Sharkey	9	Terry Alcock
Johnny Crossan	10	Jimmy Hill
George Mulhall	11	Bill Punton

Sharkey 35, 40, 44, 60, 86 Anderson 57, Crossan 66	**Scorers**	Hill 85

Referee: A Holland

WHEN KEVIN PHILLIPS was playing for Sunderland I used to worry every time he scored four goals in a game. I always want Sunderland to win and win well, but I quite like being the only man alive who can claim to have scored five goals in a game for the club. I was only nineteen at the time and I'd only recently replaced Brian Clough in the team. Cloughie was some act to follow, he'd scored 28 goals in 28 games that season until he was horribly injured in a game against Bury on Boxing Day. I was given his number nine shirt and played my first game in over a year three days after Brian's injury in the reverse fixture against Bury, a game we lost 3-0.

I'd first come into the team in 1960 and had four goals in seven games to my name when I got the chance to play regularly. The Norwich game was my fifth game since coming into the side and I hadn't scored. I made up for it, though, with five goals in a 7-1 win and while, after a performance like that, you'd expect the senior players to be delighted for you they seemed to be even more pleased than I might have expected.

I didn't know at the time, but the senior players were on a bonus based on their league position at certain points in the season and this was one of them. Len Ashurst and myself still joke about it, because the senior players got around £1,000 each after that result, which was a lot of money in those days and all I got was the ball! The bonus wasn't in my contract. We won the game 7-1 and I was happy getting the ball at the time. Through the years, though, the ball is worth more to me than the money, so it's a joke now, but was serious at the time!

The opening goal of the Norwich game didn't come until ten minutes before half-time, but by the time we went in at the break I'd scored a hat trick. It was one of the quickest a Sunderland player has ever scored and, although Roker Park was open for another 34 years, I don't think anyone ever scored a quicker one there for Sunderland after that.

Johnny Crossan and George Herd were both skilful players and they opened Norwich up to put me through for the first goal and I just closed my eyes and lashed it! For the second one I got onto the end of a pass from Jim McNab, I ran from the half-way line. I was waiting for the centre-half Ashman to try and pick me up, so at the last minute I just ran across into the penalty area and smashed it in. For the third, Sandy Kennon, the South African who was in goal for Norwich, came flying out to try and cut out one of George Mulhall's left wing crosses, but I got there first with a diving header.

By now we were full of confidence, we were just running into a bit of form. Johnny Crossan had scored a hat-trick in the previous game and we just kept scoring in the second half. Again it was a blitz of three goals in ten minutes and this time all three goals came from corners. Stan Anderson headed in one from George Mulhall, Johnny Crossan netted one from a Jimmy Davison corner and in between them I got one. Whenever we got a corner in those days Charlie Hurley used to stride up from the back and defences could get quite panicky about having him around the box. Charlie thumped a header goalwards from Jimmy's corner and I had my back to goal, but threw myself at it and managed to get a head to it from about six yards out. I remember that one very well.

Norwich got a consolation late on through Jimmy Hill [Not the bearded wonder of Fulham and Coventry fame], but we went straight up the other end and scored again ourselves. I used to get a lot of goals off George Mulhall. He would cut in from the left and lash in powerful shots, which goalkeepers couldn't hold. As he shaped to shoot I'd know that there'd more than likely be a rebound coming my way and I'd know which angle it was going to spill out at from the keeper, so I'd be there ready to say thanks very much and tap them in. And that was exactly what happened. I was left with an easy tap in for my fifth.

Having scored five goals in a match is something I'm proud of to this day. I was used to scoring goals. I'd scored a lot as a young lad. My best season was obviously for the Sunderland juniors, but I only played a season in that team, then I was in the reserves and eventually the first team. I scored 187 goals altogether in my first season for the juniors. That is a lot.

There was a kids programme on the TV, which had Danny Blanchflower on it. I can't remember what it was called, but he mentioned my name on this programme, simply for the fact that I hadn't scored in a game. There was one game when I never scored and he mentioned it on television! He said, "he's scored so many goals this season and he hasn't scored today." Typical! The most I scored in one game was 13 against Scunthorpe and it turned out they were the team I made my first team debut against. I was only a 16 year-old when I was promoted into the first team. Up to that point I was the youngest forward ever to play for the club.

I'll always remember the Norwich match for the five goals I scored, but another match that lives in my memory just as much was a game against Benfica. It was a friendly in name only. Benfica had been in the last three European Cup Finals and had won two of them. They were touring England in the middle of our season and the games were taken extremely seriously. They had played Stoke City first and hammered them 5-1. Stoke were in the First Division with players like Peter Dobing, Jimmy McIlroy and Stanley Matthews, while we were in the Second. Benfica came up to Sunderland on a Wednesday night in November 1963. We played under the lights, which always made for a good atmosphere and there were 43,000 excited fans there. The Portuguese had all the stars, Eusebio and co, and we gave them a good hammering 5-3.

I scored a hat-trick and I remember every one of the goals. The first was a ball that put me clean through, I drove it with my left foot and it went in the left corner. I thought, "this is it", because in those days, once I'd got a goal you couldn't stop me. I was after my second. That came from close range and the third was when George Mulhall ran through and whacked the ball, and I thought the goalkeeper was going to palm it out. He did, so I just followed it up and stuck it in.

It was great to get a hat-trick against such opposition, but the best goal I scored in that game was the one they didn't give me. Somebody crossed it in from the right and I volleyed in from 20 yards – into the top corner, but it was chalked off because someone was offside. It would have been allowed these days. The ones that counted were ordinary goals.

A couple of months later I got another hat-trick in the League against Swindon at Roker and I can remember a couple of those. One was special. From a throw in at the Roker End, I let it run across me and whacked it from 25 yards – it flew in because the wind was behind me. It looked better than it probably would have without the wind, there was a hell of a wind blowing that day. The other goal I remember from that day was another one following up a Mulhall shot. He let one fly from about 20 yards and I knew the keeper would palm it out and I was there.

I used to get most of my goals from poaching them in the box, but I scored a few spectacular ones as well. I'll always remember one against Manchester United. I even have a photograph of it in my front room – a perfect overhead kick. A couple of weeks after my hat-trick against Swindon we beat Everton in the Fifth round of the FA Cup and drew Manchester United at Old Trafford in the quarter-final. They were the Cup holders, but we were a good team on the way to winning promotion and we should have won. We were well ahead – 3-1 up with four minutes to go. Half of our supporters were three quarters of the way home. Jimmy Montgomery got injured, but jumped up too quickly. He should have stayed down until he was okay, but he was concussed and we couldn't reorganise, so we lost two late goals to draw 3-3.

The second game was at Roker Park – I scored that spectacular goal early on and we held out for donkeys. It looked as if we were going to win until there was another late fiasco. Bobby Charlton scored with a header on the six-yard line, so it ended up after extra-time 2-2, but we should have won it. We went to Huddersfield for the second replay. We were six inches deep in mud and I did the wrong thing again, I scored the first goal. That really got United's gander up, so they lashed us 5-1. Manchester Untied were a great team and when they finished us off, they finished us off right and proper. Having said that, in two of the three games we should have beaten them. The third game was their game.

That goal against Manchester United at Roker was one of my best, but I've scored a few from 20 to 25 yards. Some of them stick in my mind, one was against Huddersfield. I played against a guy called John Coddington, who was a big ginger-headed hit man, who gave me a few bruises. It gave me great joy to turn around and stick it in from 25 yards right in the top corner at Roker Park!

One of the best goals I've ever scored was against Blackburn. I was up against centre-half Mike England, who went on to star for Spurs, and got the ball 25 yards out. I saw him coming, so I thought, "I'm going to hit this," and it screamed it into the top corner. Fred Ellis was the goalkeeper. Another good one came against Everton – Brian Labone was the centre-half – great man, sorely missed since his death in May 2006. I dummied it past him and stuck it in the top corner again. Memories like that you always retain.

These days you can get videos and DVDs of goals just by one player, but unfortunately there's not many of my goals on film. I used to play golf with someone who was on local telly, he said there was a load of gear there that he could have got with me on, but he never ever did it. I've got a few of my goals on film, there's the history of Sunderland video and the Benfica goals are on there, but not the Norwich game – and that bugs me. The one against Manchester United is on. I watch it quite a lot.

From coming into the team until we got promoted in 1964 my manager was Alan Brown. I have different feelings about him – he was a great coach, but as a manager I didn't rate him. He really was fantastic coach – ahead of his time, but that bonus I missed out on the night I scored five times annoyed me. He'd also got me to sign professional forms without my father there – I was only 15, and I could have got a signing on fee – he knew that, so he got me to sign the form before my father came. He'd do things like that.

My father had played against Alan Brown. My Dad, Colin, was in the RAF and Browny was in the Army and they played opposite each other in a representative game. Dad was centre-forward and Browny, a defender, kicked seven bells out of him! My dad also used to play alongside Sunderland's physio, Johnny Watters. Johnny went on to have a great career as a player with Celtic. Dad had played with Johnny for a season. Johnny was a 16 year-old kid and he was farmed out to junior teams and one of them was my dad's team, St. Rocks – Johnny was inside-left, while my Dad played outside-left, although Dad was a lot older than Johnny.

One day my Dad came down to see me play. He used to ride down from Scotland on his Vespa scooter to watch me. It was a surprise when they saw each other – it was about 40 years after they'd played together, just after I'd come down to Wearside as a kid – and they met. Johnny went, "I know you," and that was it, they were off. Johnny was at Sunderland for years and years working for many different managers.

Alan Brown left after we won promotion. We had just missed out in the two previous seasons. It was fantastic when we beat Charlton to go up purely and simply because the previous year, we'd lost a game against Chelsea which was a game we should never have lost. It was our last game of the season and we only needed a draw to go up. We lost it and that was it. Chelsea went up instead on goal average. Tommy Docherty put a special team out. Hit men like the Harris brothers. They kicked Charlie Hurley all over the place and it worked for them on the day, so it was doubly pleasing to win the game against Charlton.

We started the first season after promotion without a manager and we didn't get one until November! With having no manager, the run of results weren't very clever [one win in the first 15 League games]. Arthur Wright and Jackie Jones did their best as our trainers, but for me, the man running the team was Charlie Hurley. He actually turned around and said, "forget what these two guys are telling you – I'll do the business." He went to see the directors. Then we all just gelled together and went out to fight for the team, and we got out of relegation trouble no bother.

George Hardwick came and went as manager in 1964/65. George was a lovely man. Some of the things he did were remarkable. Once we were playing a cup-tie against Nottingham Forest at home. George had had some guy watching them. George came into the dressing room and got this big document out. Going through the team he said, "Goalkeeper: terrible at crosses, crap" and he goes through the team going on about all these well-known players. He came to Terry Hennessy and he goes, "this team's crap," so he ripped the document up. They beat us 3-1, so that was it – he never did that again!

I finished top scorer that season with 21 goals in 35 games. It was ten more than anyone else scored, but once a new manager was appointed in the summer of 1965 I knew I'd be leaving. That was because the new manager the board appointed to replace Hardwick was Ian McColl.

McColl had been manager of Scotland when I'd been called up a couple of years earlier. In those days it was a group of selectors who picked the squad, not the manager. I got called up to a squad with Jimmy Johnstone the great Celtic winger. When Jimmy and I arrived at Ayr to train, McColl turned around and said, "I don't know what you two are doing here." At the time we looked up and laughed, but I knew then we wouldn't be selected for the full team – and we went back to our clubs.

But then a few weeks later he was appointed as Sunderland manager. He saw me and said, "I don't want you here." That's true. The thing is, when he was appointed manager, I knew I was gone right away. I knew my time was up. I kept playing in the team and I kept scoring, but he made it evident he didn't want me. The directors couldn't believe it.

People don't believe me when I tell the full story, there's a lot more to it. He'd spent fifteen years playing for Rangers and I was a Catholic. That is the truth. Check how many Catholic players transferred from Sunderland when he joined. Mike Hellawell, Harry Hood, John O'Hare – just check. Three quarters of the players who left were Catholics. People don't believe me – but it's the God's honest truth.

I put in a transfer request. I'd been tapped to go elsewhere, so I asked for a transfer and he called me up on the Friday and said, "you've got one of four teams – Norwich City, Leicester City, Wolverhampton and Blackpool" That was my choice and he said, "Don't effing well come back." Those were his words.

I left to go to Leicester – they were in the top six in the First Division and had Gordon Banks in goal. My record at Leicester was better than at Sunderland where I averaged better than one goal every two games. I scored every one and a half games of the handful of games I had for Leicester, but I had a bad injury and that wrecked me.

I always thought I'd do really well playing alongside a good target man and the main reason I signed for Leicester was to partner Derek Dougan. He played one game alongside me – against Manchester United – and was transferred the next week! I've often wondered what could have happened if I could have played with a target man. I'd have loved to have been able to do what Kevin Phillips did at Sunderland and play alongside Niall Quinn. I would have loved to have played with Quinny, he was a fantastic player.

I did, of course, play with some tremendous players at Sunderland. Charlie was amazing and Stan Anderson was a great character. They were all characters, but Charlie, Stan and John Crossan stand out for different reasons. Thinking back, Crossan was always behind most of the laughs. We once stayed at a hotel when Stanley Ritson was a one of the directors, In those days you used to put your shoes outside the room to get cleaned. Johnny's idea of fun would be to switch all the shoes. Stanley used to wear brown boots which Johnny hid, so poor Stanley came down in the morning with just his socks. Then Johnny stuck his boots in the pond in the middle of the garden. Somebody fished them out in the end. Typical Johnny Crossan.

I'm a member of Sunderland's Former Players' Association. It's thriving. There are new members coming all the time. I've met a few guys who I played junior football with at Sunderland – I never thought I'd ever see them again. I love it because you're in contact with the players you spent your earlier life with.

In recent years I've been selling and renting fruit machines and pool tables for a living. My region covers most of the north east. I meet a lot of people who remember me. They like to talk about football, I like to talk about football – I thoroughly enjoy it.

I played for Mansfield and Hartlepool after Leicester. I played for Len Ashurst at Hartlepool, but he sacked me and likes to remind me about it when I play golf with him now! The thing is, I'd have loved nothing better to have spent all my career at Sunderland. I came here as a 15 year-old kid and I live in Sunderland now, not far from Roker Park. I love the north east area. I had six years in the Midlands and never really settled. If McColl hadn't come to Sunderland I would have finished my career here – because I hadn't lost my touch – I was still scoring goals.

LEN ASHURST
LEFT-BACK 1957–1971

BORN   10 March 1939, Liverpool
SIGNED   27 December 1957 from Prescott Cables
SUNDERLAND CAREER   452(6) games, 4 goals
HONOURS   Promotion from Division Two 1963/64
LEFT   Free transfer to Hartlepool United, 8th March 1971
RETURNED AS MANAGER   5 March 1984 to 24th May 1985

Len Ashurst has made more appearances for Sunderland than any other outfield player and is one of only four former stars to manage the club. Known as 'Lennie the Lion,' Ashurst was tough, tenacious and talented. Ever present in Sunderland's first ever promotion season of 1963/64, Len missed a mere two games between April 1960 and November 1964. A lengthy managerial career included spells with the national teams of Kuwait, Qatar and Malaysia. In 2006 he was still working for the Premier League as a match assessor.

Manchester United 3 v Sunderland 3

FA Cup Sixth Round
Saturday 29 February 1964

Old Trafford
Attendance 61,700

*Promotion-bound Sunderland see Cup holders United score two late
goals to force the first of two replays in an FA Cup epic*

Teams

Matt Busby	**Managers**	Alan Brown
David Gaskell	1	Jimmy Montgomery
Shay Brennan	2	Cecil Irwin
Tony Dunne	3	Len Ashurst
Pat Crerand	4	Martin Harvey
Bill Foulkes	5	Charlie Hurley
Maurice Setters	6	Colin Nelson
Nobby Stiles	7	Brian Usher
Denis Law	8	George Herd
David Herd	9	Nick Sharkey
Bobby Charlton	10	Johnny Crossan
George Best	11	George Mulhall

Hurley (og) 55, Charlton 86 **Scorers** Mulhall 43, Crossan 49, pen 60
Best 87

Referee: A Holland

THE TITANIC FA CUP quarter-final against Manchester United is the game I would pick as the 'Match of My Life' simply because it was a terrific match, which led on to two other fantastic contests. Until over half-way through the third game we were still clinging on to the hope that we might get a Wembley place.

Wembley was on our lips because the draw came out on the Monday after the first game and it matched the winner of our tie up with West Ham. We would have really fancied our chances against the Hammers because they were a football team and we were quite tough as a group of lads. I played in the Under 23s for England with their skipper Bobby Moore and when I met Bobby later that season, he said to me, "We didn't want to play you because you were the only unknown quantity to us, we knew Man United and we wanted to play them."

We knew very well that if we had have played West Ham we probably would've gone through to the Final where we would have had Preston or Swansea, who were the other semi-finalists. They were both Second Division clubs like ourselves, so there was a golden opportunity there which was missed purely by the events of two or three remarkable minutes at the end of the first game against Manchester United – and not far off that length of time in the second match as well.

Manchester United were the current FA Cup holders, having beaten Leicester 3-1 in the 1963 Final and the three games against them produced sixteen goals. They were highly entertaining matches, which is no doubt one of the reasons why they live in the supporters' and players' memories. For me the tie was something special. Looking back at the first game at Old Trafford, you think we were so close to beating them as we were 3-1 up with about five minutes to go. Everyone remembers Monty getting a head injury. Now, in present day football, Monty would have probably been substituted and a replacement goalkeeper put in, but with substitutes in British football still some two years off, that wasn't an option. With hindsight the trainer should have told Monty to lie there quite a lot longer then he did so he could recover. Monty usually collected everything in the six yard box, but when play re-started it was a corner to Man United.

Some shrewd player on the opposition said "Listen, stick it under the bar and we'll put the ball and Monty in the back of the net." Bobby Charlton beat everybody to it and headed the second goal, which then led to the third one a few minutes later which frustrated me because it was scored by George Best. You see, I was playing against him and I always prided myself on doing quite well against George Best over the years. This was the first time, I think, that I'd ever played against him and I know that particular day I had a damn good game against him. I've got a photograph showing George Best's goal and it still bugs me really because he hit a left foot shot. He was normally right-footed, but hit a speculative left foot shot when he was probably 22-23 yards out; I can see it now.

The photographer took this snap from behind where George took the shot. He must have been sitting somewhere between the half-way line and the corner flag and the picture shows the ball had actually gone through several different players on both sides and crept into the bottom corner. Monty was obviously unsighted and possibly still struggling to focus because of the incident three minutes beforehand, but this ball had actually gone through the legs of one of those players and I think it was big Charlie Hurley. I'm not sure, but in the photo there we are, all looking back following the ball – Besty, myself, there's Charlie Hurley and another Man United player and then there's that bloody ball going into the bottom of the net. And that sticks in the gullet because it should never have got there really, but that's the way it goes. It was 3-3 and United had come back from the dead. I suppose that's what had made them Cup winners the year before.

That's a very, very clear image of the tumultuous end of the game Overall it was a lovely sunny day, there was a firm pitch, with over sixty thousand there and in amongst them were my Mum and Dad. It wasn't easy in those days for them to travel up and down the country to watch me play in games, especially with Dad working seven days most weeks, but he'd managed to get himself along the East Lancs Road from Liverpool to Manchester for this match because it was such a special occasion. He was at the game with Mum and my brothers, who are Liverpool supporters, but on that day they were cheering for us. When we used to play Liverpool they would cheer for Liverpool as their allegiance would never be broken. In fact it still isn't to this day with my brothers. They saw a great game and had a fantastic afternoon.

I think on the day we were the better team, I'm absolutely convinced of that. I know that we were never under pressure until maybe the second half a little bit, but generally speaking we were always on top and I think I'm correct in saying we were always in front as well.

George Mulhall got the first goal with a header and a Johnny Crossan shot put us two nil up, I can see that now. Then they pulled one back through an own goal header from Charlie Hurley. We were still the better team, though, and deserved to make it 3-1 when Johnny Crossan scored again. Johnny was nothing short of brilliant that day. He dribbled past three players before being brought down for a penalty, which he scored himself.

At 3-1 up with half an hour to go we were comfortable for a full 25 minutes until Monty was knocked out and then they got those two late goals. In my opinion they actually scored three flukey goals because the header by Bobby Charlton came as Monty was down and out, as it were, and was certainly not focused. There was the one I've mentioned from George Best that went through everybody's legs and the first one was the stunner really because we were comfortable at 2-0 and I can see big Charlie now back-heading it. I was standing alongside him more or less, because I was on the cover. Monty was about to grab it and Charlie's tried to flick it back to him, it bobbled and trickled and hardly reached the net. That was a sickener on the day. But we coped with that blow and Johnny's penalty seemed to have put us into the semi-final.

One of the reasons we were on top in the match and indeed one of the reasons why we'd had the cup run and eventually won promotion that season was that we had the two best playmakers in the country at the time in my opinion – and I'm talking about players like Johnny Haynes and Stan Anderson playing football at that time. On that particular day at Old Trafford, George Herd and Johnny Crossan were magnificent. The match was probably the best I ever saw George play, he revelled in it. Johnny was a big time player and on that particular day they couldn't cope with either of them and that was one of the main reasons why we were on top and why we played so well over the 90 minutes.

I think it was also one of the reasons in the long run why Johnny Crossan eventually ended up in Manchester, because Man City had spotted the potential in the lad. Well, the potential had already come to fruition really, but they certainly saw how good a player he was and must have thought, if he can manipulate a game against Man Utd then he's worth having and Johnny ended up at Maine Road, of course.

There had been over 60,000 at Old Trafford for the first match, but there were many thousands more at Roker Park for the replay. There were probably over 80 thousand people around the area of which maybe 75,000 got into the ground one way or another, the rest just couldn't fit in! It was desperate. We used to walk up from the Roker Hotel, where we used to have our pre-match meals. When we tried to walk up for that match the crowd was absolutely colossal.

Walking up to the ground was an important part of our pre-match build up for big games. We even used to do it at away games. Alan Brown had a habit of stopping the team coach about ten to fifteen minutes walk away from where we were playing and we'd walk up to the ground to get a feel for the atmosphere. We did that quite a number of times and I think it stemmed from the fact we had our pre-match meals for home games at the Roker Hotel generally. It changed to the Seaburn Hotel at one stage, but mainly we used The Roker. We'd leave our cars in the hotel car park and walk from there up to Roker Park. I think this was something Alan Brown wanted to follow on and, as we did it at home, we did it away quite regularly. He'd stop the bus and we'd all get off and walk along with George Curtis, one of the trainers. We'd done it for the Old Trafford match and I remember walking up Trafford Way with my colleagues Martin [Harvey] and Cecil [Irwin]. The closer we got to the ground the more we felt that we were going to do the business because the adrenalin started to pump early. There were loads of Sunderland supporters and they were really with us, it was brilliant. By the time we reached the ground we were up for it. It certainly helped us. That was another very vivid memory of that particular match

My father-in-law came to the replay an hour and a half before kick-off and he was just carried along by the crowds. He told me there were people in the car park outside the main gate, who had to stand on the bonnets and roofs of cars to get away from the crush. It was a miracle really that it wasn't a huge catastrophe quite frankly. That particular night they just didn't expect a gate to be so big. You know they underestimated the north east people – they could see us getting to Wembley that year.

I know from the people who looked after the ticket office then that they had a major problem. There used to be a little ticket office where you picked up tickets. A friend of mine popped his head out a couple of hours before kick-off and told me all he could see was an absolute mass of faces all standing for tickets. It was a desperate situation because they didn't have a ticket left. All of the tickets that had been printed had been sold, every single one had been distributed and there was a mob outside that he feared were ready to rip them apart to get into the match, so they shut the window and buggered off!

That resulted in the gates simply being broken down at the Roker End, because people were so frustrated they couldn't get in. Two people were killed. Whether they were killed in the crush or whether they died of heart attacks or whatever I don't know

I'm not sure whether the kick-off was delayed, but I know that there was an official attendance of 46,000. The irony of that particular night was that we used to get a crowd bonus of £5 each per thousand for over 55,000. Now the ground held about 62,000, but on that particular night, because the gates were broken down, there was seventy-odd thousand, so we missed a crowd bonus because of the fact that wasn't the official gate. It was interesting in so much that we didn't know how many folk were in and this particular crowd bonus had been based on those who paid. It's probably true to say that over 25,000 people got into that stadium without paying and, because of the overflow, they were pushed round the side of the pitch.

The match itself, when it started, was as good as the first contest for entertainment value and, because it went into extra-time, there was two hours of fantastic football. I can picture it again, it was a floodlit game on a fairly brisk north east evening. There were thousands of people lining the pitch on the outside perimeter. Because of the crowd, the atmosphere was fantastic on the night and, as at Old Trafford, we were more than a match for United. Like the first game we took the lead just before half-time, this time with a spectacular volley from Nick Sharkey. Two of our best players as ever were Monty and Charlie, but the irony was that, following Charlie's own goal in the first game, Monty made a mistake for their equaliser. As Jim was taking a goal kick he kicked the ground and only gave the ball to Denis Law, who slipped it into the net. So, despite the fact that Monty had played so well over the games, he was instrumental in a way in being involved in a couple of the goals we conceded.

We ended up going to extra-time again with the score at 1-1 and went back in front when Maurice Setters scored an own goal in trying to prevent George Herd having a tap-in. We held out throughout nearly all of the extra period, but right at the death Bobby Charlton scored an equaliser. There were no penalty shoot-outs back then, so it meant a second replay.

Of course we were still going for promotion, so, unlike Manchester United, we couldn't rest players from League games so they'd be fresh for the Cup. The second replay was scheduled to be at Huddersfield on the Monday night and on the Saturday we played a very tough match at home against Middlesbrough.

We got to half-time all square in the third game against Matt Busby's men, but then we took the lead yet again and it was probably a bad thing really. We went one-nil up through Nick Sharkey, but then we collapsed. I think it was down to two reasons. The pitch was very, very heavy and we didn't recover once they got the first goal straight after we'd scored. It was as if the whole of the team had sort of said, "Well stuff it!" They'd done it again, they'd got another one back. It was as if we'd never shake them off. They'd still never been ahead in the tie and I think mentally we collapsed on that particular night. It's funny how I don't remember it so well. The only thing I can really recollect about that game was another huge crowd, another floodlit game and another fantastic atmosphere and us playing quite well actually until they scored their first goal.

I do remember that my brother had been married a few days previously and he came up for the match. I had a couple of tickets, but Dad couldn't come because he was working. So my two Liverpool-supporting brothers came along and one of them had a piece of wedding cake from his wedding. When I saw him afterwards the newly-wed explained that the crowd was so huge and they were jam packed in so tightly he'd had to take the wedding cake out of his pocket and hold it above his head for the whole game and, of course, everyone kept asking him what was in the box. He was determined to give me the piece of cake. I do recollect that little personal note on that particular game.

We went out of the Cup, but the consolation was we went on to win promotion. Alan Brown had built a great team. You ask any of the players that played in the '64 team. Some of them will reluctantly acknowledge that he was good for them and the majority would most definitely acknowledge the fact that Alan Brown set their careers up. He set us on our way and we enjoyed playing under him. When we look back it was rigid discipline which was instilled into us. He was a character builder and he had oceans of character himself. Out of that team or the players that passed through his hands at Sunderland you could probably name two dozen who went on to either manage in football, coach football at a good level or retained a connection to the game in some capacity or other. That to me was a great testimony to Alan Brown's stature.

It stemmed from the fact that he employed discipline and, while some players didn't like it, generally speaking they would admit that it definitely worked. I would be in the most definite category. I learnt a lot from him and I think one of the other people who was an advocate of Alan Brown's philosophy and attitude in approaching footballers was Brian Clough. He applied that philosophy himself and look where it got him, so Browny for me was ahead of his time as a coach.

Alan was one of the head coaches of the FA. I went on courses that he was in charge of, so there was a situation where it was the manager and the player going on a course at Lilleshall. I was lucky in that I was able to learn so much from him. He introduced shadow play to the game. We all used shadow play to drill our players when we went on to manage clubs and shadow play still exists in football today. It's a way of organising your team and the way that you play. You play with eleven players against nobody, with the idea being that nobody can break things down, so you get what you are aiming for actually spot on.

The biggest mistake the directors ever made was to let Alan Brown go. He left after winning promotion and it was a huge loss. I look back and think, if we had retained Alan Brown, more than likely we would have brought more players in and been successful. Leeds went up along with us, beating us to the Second Division Championship by one point, although we'd had a win and a draw against them that season. Yet three or four months into the new season we were bottom and they were top, they went into Europe, reached the FA Cup Final that season and went on to be very successful as one of the dominant sides of the era.

Strangely it was a disaster when we won promotion. I heard from an ex-director that Alan Brown left in the summer because he never got the same bonuses as the players. It wasn't in written into his contract and Brown was never a man to ask for anything, he would just shake hands on the deal and that would be it.

He left Roker Park to go to Sheffield Wednesday – he took them to the FA Cup Final two years later and left us in the lurch incidentally – because of the bonus issue. We'd got a bonus, he hadn't so he upped and left. Then they made the biggest mistake any board of directors could ever make by appointing George Crow as the man in charge of the contracts and so on! Now whether Football League rules said that you have to have a manager I'm not sure. George never ever pulled a tracksuit on because he was an accountant and they put the two trainers Jack Jones and Arthur Wright in charge of the team. We went from the start of the season right through to November before they appointed George Hardwick as manager; but not until after we'd plummeted to the very bottom of the league. Alan Brown's departure right after we'd won promotion was a huge shock to us, it was a huge mistake and a bad, bad decision.

George Hardwick was the opposite of Alan Brown. He was a man who used to enjoy the fruits of life, he was a gregarious, whole-hearted handsome chap. He came in, gathered us round and said, "just go out and play." Some of our players blossomed. I was one of them, being a left-back, the position in which George Hardwick of England stature had played for Great Britain. He allowed me a little bit more freedom than Alan Brown used to. I was told that I played some of my best football with George Hardwick and I think that as well.

The sad part about George Hardwick was that he came in when we were bottom of the table and he took us to fifteenth in a league of twenty two at the end of the season, but then got the sack. There was no logic in that, no logic whatsoever.

An annual event for us was to go to London at the end of the season, go to the Café Royal, have a meal on the Friday and go to the FA Cup Final on the Saturday. At the Café Royal the Sunderland chairman Syd Collings stood up and thanked George Hardwick for his great effort in taking us from bottom to safety and said he had done a fantastic job. We got back home on the Monday and discovered that the board had sacked him for non-football reasons.

If it had been a disaster to let Alan Brown go the previous summer it was another disaster to appoint Ian McColl to replace George Hardwick. McColl was a disaster for me and for a number of other players. It's no coincidence that quite a number of the Catholic players were released and drifted out of the club. McColl had played for Rangers and was a Rangers man. You can't tell me that the likes of Jimmy McNab, Nicky Sharkey and Charlie Hurley were surplus to requirements.

Ian McColl was really not good for a number of the players from the promotion side because of the fact that he brought in Jim Baxter. Baxter was a fantastic player, a superb talent, but there was always going to be a rift between Baxter and Hurley and the Hurley regime of players, so the dressing room was immediately split. There was the Scotsman and the 'Proddy dogs' and then there was the Alan Brown/Charlie Hurley contingent, who were against the principle of what Ian McColl stood for. He was a man of few words and he managed that way. To me that was a bad appointment, although some would say it was a good appointment because they flourished under him, but, for me, McColl was a total disaster for the club. He certainly didn't move it forward as Sunderland never finished any higher than that 15th position in the First Division during his reign.

I eventually left to join Hartlepool in 1971 just before my thirty-second birthday. By then Alan Brown had returned to Roker Park for a second spell and the club had, once again, sadly, been relegated. I began my managerial career at Hartlepool and took charge of Gillingham, Sheffield Wednesday, Newport County and Cardiff City before becoming manager of Sunderland.

Not many people know this, but I actually had Testimonial matches at three clubs. I had one at Newport – who I reached the quarter-final of the European Cup Winners' Cup with only to lose narrowly to Carl Zeiss Jena over two legs. I had one at Cardiff and as a player I had one at Sunderland. Unfortunately I didn't get much of a crowd at my game at Sunderland. The game had been meant to take place at the end of the previous season, which would have been great because we were playing Newcastle and they had just won the Fairs Cup, but because of their involvement in that the match was delayed and delayed. We eventually played it in the November of 1969 and by time it came round we were struggling.

My recollection of my 18-20 months as manager of Sunderland was one of mixed feelings really as we reached the League Cup Final at Wembley in 1984/85, only to lose narrowly to Norwich with a deflected goal, but were relegated. To some extent I had the same sort of problems as managers had suffered from in my day as a player in that when I came in I had a number of players who were behind the previous manager and I had that with Alan Durban's group of players.

After Sunderland I managed all over the place, Kuwait, Qatar, became assistant manager at Blackpool and then went back to Cardiff. I had spells in charge at Weymouth and Weston-Super-Mare and, in between, did a stint coaching for the national side in Malaysia.

Since 1998 I've been involved with the FA Premier League, overseeing the development of the Academy system across the country and also being a Premier League match delegate responsible for assessing everything about what happens at a club on a match day and reporting back to the powers that be on what has gone well and what could be improved. I've been in the game over fifty years and without doubt the best of those times were at Sunderland and especially in that tremendous side of the early sixties. If only we could have held on for those last couple of minutes at Old Trafford and we could have had an FA Cup/promotion double.

CHARLIE HURLEY
CENTRE-HALF 1957–1969

BORN   4 October 1936, Cork
SIGNED   26 September 1957 from Millwall; £18,000
SUNDERLAND CAREER   401 games, 26 goals
HONOURS   Promotion from Division Two 1963/64, Runner-up to Bobby Moore as Footballer of the Year 1964, Sunderland AFC's Player of the Century
LEFT   Free transfer to Bolton Wanderers, 2 June 1969

Voted Sunderland's Player of the Century by fans in the club's Centenary year of 1979, Charlie Hurley is known to this day as 'The King' on Wearside. A colossus of a centre-half, Hurley was the first defender to start coming forward at set pieces, something football the world over takes for granted nowadays. Supremely powerful in the air, Hurley was a talented footballing defender and a natural leader. He captained the club to its first ever promotion and in the following year, when the club didn't have a manager until November, it was Charlie who effectively called the shots with the players.

Sunderland 2 v Charlton Athletic 1

League Division Two
Saturday 18 April 1964

Rokr Park
Attendance 50,827

Charlie captains the Lads to a first ever promotion after two near misses

Teams

	Alan Brown	**Managers**	Frank Hill
	Jimmy Montgomery	1	Peter Wakeham
	Cecil Irwin	2	John Hewie
	Len Ashurst	3	Brian Kinsey
	Martin Harvey	4	Mike Bailey
	Charlie Hurley	5	Brian Tocknell
	Jimmy McNab	6	Dennis Edwards
	Brian Usher	7	Roy Matthews
	George Herd	8	Keith Peacock
	Nick Sharkey	9	Mike Kenning
	Johnny Crossan	10	Eddie Firmani
	George Mulhall	11	Len Glover

	Herd 43, Crossan 89	**Scorers**	Firmani 17

Referee: W Crossley

NERVES WERE A MASSIVE problem for us on the day that we won promotion by beating Charlton in 1964. In my day only the top two teams in the Second Division won promotion. The Play-offs didn't exist. We had finished third two seasons running and had just missed out. In 1963 we'd only needed to draw our last game of the season at home to Chelsea to go up, but we blew it as they won 1-0 to pip us to second spot on goal average and so, as we prepared to take on Charlton, we were thinking, "Is it going to be third time lucky or unlucky?" Until 1958 Sunderland held the record as the only team never to have played outside the top flight. I'd joined them from Millwall during the 1957/58 campaign, but we went down that season and had been trying ever since to get back.

I was a pretty cool customer, but even I was nervous as we got ready. I didn't show it, though, because as captain I had to lead by example. We had a lot of young players and I went round talking to them one by one in the dressing room before the match. We had lads like Cecil Irwin, Len Ashurst and Jimmy McNab. We were a bunch of great friends, not just team-mates. We saw a lot of each other socially. None of us were boozers or smokers, but we spent a lot of time together and we were really up for it.

Alan Brown was the best manager ever to be in charge of me and he was a very strong person, but on the day we played Charlton he was different, so I knew he was worried too. There were over 50,000 fans there and that can be quite frightening when you know their hopes hang on you. At one point in the early sixties we went a year and a half without losing at home and a large part of that was down to the fans, to the Roker Roar, but the level of expectation was so high and we just didn't want to let anyone down, so we were a bundle of nerves that day.

In those days the players were very, very close to the fans. We used to have lunch at the Roker Hotel at the sea front and then walk up to the ground in amongst the fans. The camaraderie was tremendous. The fans were mainly miners and shipyard workers, so they weren't slow in telling us exactly what we should do with the opposition. You could always tell a miner because no matter how much they washed they could never get all of the coal out of their hands or their fingernails. It was ingrained in them just like supporting Sunderland was. They were lovely people, people I'll never forget. We had the jitters because of the previous year when we'd lost to Chelsea and we knew the supporters couldn't take another disappointment like that. We still had one game left to play, away at Grimsby, so it wasn't last chance saloon, but it was a great opportunity to seal promotion in front of our own fans, who had been so disappointed the previous two years.

Those jitters got worse when we went 1-0 down early on when Eddie Firmani scored and, in fact, we could easily have been two down before we got the equaliser. Our old goalkeeper Peter Wakeham was playing for Charlton and he was having a terrific game. I went close a couple of times myself with headers from corner-kicks.

I was the first centre-half to go forward for corners. A lot of people think it was Alan Brown that got me to go forward, but it wasn't, it was Stan Anderson. Stan was the captain and one day we were playing against Sheffield United when we got a corner and Stan said, "Go on up and they'll wonder what's hit them!" It proved to be true. I was pretty good in the air and I caused havoc! The idea of a centre-half moving forward was brand new and I scored. Centre-halves never went up for corners or free-kicks until then, but afterwards it became an absolute must. I scored 26 goals for Sunderland and for a defender that was a total I became very proud of. Me going forward for a corner became an important part of our attacking play and it became folklore in the north east. Whenever we got a corner or a free-kick near the box the chant would go up right around the ground, "Charlie! Charlie!" and in those days crowds didn't really chant or sing in the way they do now.

I could really thump it with my head and I took a few stitches in the head to prove it! The fans and my team mates loved it when I went forward and I loved hearing the crowd shout my name. If I started playing football for Sunderland as a young lad tomorrow I'd want to be a centre forward. The greatest kick you get in football is scoring a goal. You can play badly for 89 minutes, but if you score in the other minute you are the hero!

It became par for the course for me to go up and if ever I didn't, the crowd would chant for me to do so. Even if I didn't score I'd have two or three men on me, so I'd always cause a distraction and this created a lot of goals apart from the ones I scored myself. Our centre-forward in the promotion team was Nicky Sharkey. He was like greased lightning and when I went forward he'd stick close by me. If I got a touch to the ball, he'd be there in a flash to finish it off.

Anyway in the Charlton match I was going forward at every opportunity as we tried to increase the pressure on their goal and thankfully we got that bit of luck that you need when you're in that kind of position and the crowd are just getting a bit restless when we managed to get an equaliser just before half-time. George Herd got it, finishing off a pass from Martin Harvey. It struck Charlton's defender Brian Tocknell and looped over Peter Wakeham.

In the second half we pushed and pushed for a winner and, as in the first period, the reward for our efforts came right at the end of the half as the pressure built of the Charlton defence. There was only a minute or two left when Johnny Crossan got the winner. That lifted the tension and almost straight away the final whistle went and we knew we were promoted. The amazing sense of relief was incredible. We'd finished third and third and now we had guaranteed second place we could breathe easily.

It really was a fantastic day. We did a lap of honour and went back to the dressing rooms, but we could still hear this unbelievable noise from outside. The Chairman Syd Collings came in and said, "You'll have to go out again lads." We were all half dressed and about to get into the bath, but we went out again. The roars of "Charlie! Charlie!" were fantastic and so the rest of the team lifted me onto their shoulders – which was no mean feat – and chaired me around the pitch. It will always go down as the greatest day of my footballing career, and I played from when I was seventeen until I was thirty five so that says it all.

Even now when I meet Sunderland supporters they talk about that day. Even people who weren't even born then want to talk about it because they've heard about it, the stories are passed down from one generation to the next and it is simply fantastic.

We had a great team. Lennie Ashurst, 'The Lion', and Mac the Knife [Jimmy McNab] were a very hard left flank. Lennie wasn't a dirty player; he was fair, but really hard and tenacious. Alan Brown always used to say to us, "If you make a bad tackle walk away sideways, so that the ref doesn't see your number. That way you'll be able to get away with another one later on." There were no fairies playing for Alan Brown! He always gave youngsters a chance and he got rid of all of the expensive players that were at the club before he came.

On my right-hand side we had Cecil Irwin and in front of him Stan Anderson, and then Martin Harvey after Stan left, so we had a very good right flank as well. In goal Monty was the best shot stopper in the business even though he was very young, so our defence was a really strong one. Up

Sunderland's record crowd of 75,118 saw the 1933 FA Cup
clash with Derby County.

Bobby Gurney (left) with
author Rob Mason.

Bobby's daughter Dorothy Bates with
former Sunderland Vice-Chairman John
Fickling unveiling a plaque to Bobby in his
birthplace of Silksworth in March 2006.

Mapson (goal)   Hall (left-back)   Collin (left-back)   Gorman (right-back)   McNab (left-half)   Hastings (left-half)   Johnston (centre-half)

Thomson (right-half)   Burbanks (outside-left)   Gallacher (inside-left)   Gurney (centre-forward)   Carter (inside-right)   Duns (outside-right)

Sunderland

SUNDERLAND have a proud record in the League— the Cup has always eluded them. Since 1913 a bottle of beer has been hoarded at the local Trade Union Club to drink Sunderland's Cup success in ——. Will the bottle be broached this year?

The Cup heroes of 1937, who brought the trophy to Wearside.

Bobby equalises against Preston in the 1937 FA Cup Final. It was Sunderland's first ever FA Cup final goal and the Lads went on to win 3-1.

I captained every side I played for and it was always an honour.

My first goal against Arsenal was a simple header from a corner.

That's me (left) in 2006 with Albert Snell, who had a few games
at left-half in the fifties.

That's me in 1963 with the Roker End behind me.

I've still got the ball I scored five goals against Norwich with.

That's me on my debut against Ipswich in 1958.

4/- to get into Old Trafford is the equivalent of 20p now but it was a lot of money in those days.

This is from my scrapbook.
It's George Mulhall's goal: the first of six in the 'Match of My Life'.

Another from my scrapbook, but not a happy memory,
Charlie Hurley's own goal has just made it 1-1.

When Johnny Crossan tucked away his penalty to make it 3-1 we were
convinced we'd go on to win.

Straight from the corner following Monty's injury Bobby Charlton scored one of his rare headed goals to make it 2-3, but we were still ahead with four minutes to go.

This was the sickener. I'd had a good game marking George Best but his last minute shot went through a forest of legs to creep in and make it 3-3.

This is a famous picture of me challenging Denis Law in the replay.

You can see how packed the crowds were at Roker Park,
I loved playing there.

We'd been well and truly battered at Norwich in an FA Cup
fifth round tie in 1961, but this is the moment when I headed one
of my best ever goals. It was a late winner as we won 1-0.

We were such a bunch of great friends and the Lads carried me around
Roker Park when we clinched promotion in 1964.

That's me on the shoulders of Jimmy McNab, 'Mac the Knife'
I used to call him.

The four ever presents from the 1963/64 promotion team.
(left to right) George Mulhall, Jimmy Montgomery, Len 'The Lion'
Ashurst and Johnny Crossan. I missed one game that season –
a home defeat by Southampton.

JIMMY MONTGOMERY – 1973
LEEDS UNITED 0 v SUNDERLAND 1

My view of Ian Porterfield's goal in the 1973 FA Cup Final.

Everyone else's view of the second half of my 'double' save from
Trevor Cherry and Peter Lorimer.

Wee Bobby Kerr lifts up the trophy.

Billy Hughes and I show off the FA Cup.

Bob Stokoe ran straight to me at the final whistle.
There's a statue to him at the Stadium of Light now showing
him running towards me with his arms outstretched.

Some people think I only played in the box, but I was in midfield
most of the time!

I might look calm as I complete my hat trick with a penalty at St. James',
but I was anything but calm because I knew if I missed they'd get a lift,
get back in the game...and it would be my fault.

These days I summarise on all Sunderland games for Magic 1152.

Scoring against Peter Shilton within a couple of minutes of my
Sunderland debut got me off to the perfect start in the north east.

My header in the last minute of the Play-off with Gillingham took the
game to extra-time, but we ended up being relegated on away goals!

Another Play-off disappointment, this time in the 1990 Final against Swindon at Wembley, but we ended up being promoted when Swindon were punished for financial irregularities.

I played four games at Wembley for Sunderland. This was the last of them, the 1992 FA Cup Final against Liverpool, who beat us 2-0.

Newcastle labelled the 1990 Play-off a special match when they printed the tickets without knowing who they'd be playing. They didn't know how special it would turn out to be!

I'm watching the ball thinking 'It's in, It's in,' but just for a moment I was worried it would hit the post. It did go in though and it's the goal every Sunderland supporter asks me about.

The Play-off final against Swindon was a complete disaster.
We were set up all wrong.

That's me on the right [as you look] with my brother Ricardo.
We'd have loved to played together for Sunderland, but the only time
he appeared for the club, he came on as a substitute for me.

Aren't we so gorgeous in our shell suits?
(left to right) Peter Davenport, Marco Gabbiadini, Gary Bennett
and me [Tony Norman] with coach Viv Busby at the front.

We lost the Play-off Final, but still got our ticket to the top flight
through Swindon's misdemeanours.

I'd seen Alan McLoughlin's shot early, had it covered,
but then got done by a deflection.

The diving header against Chelsea was one of the best goals I scored for
Sunderland. I'm pleased it came in a game where it capped off
a performance I was really proud of.

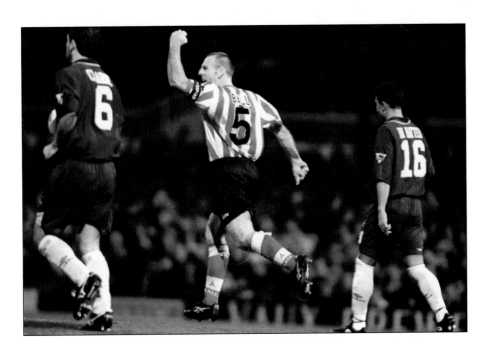

I certainly enjoyed the moment!

Ha'way the Lads!

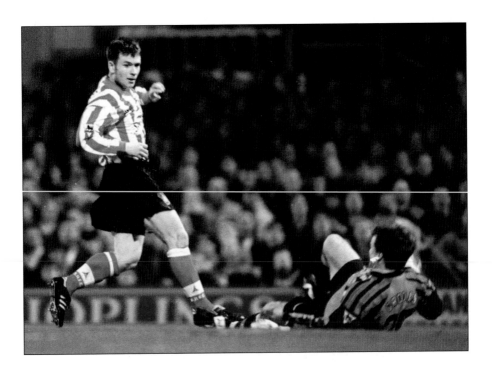

Craig Russell scored the third to seal an emphatic win.

At home with some of my shirts and medals from
big games with Sunderland.

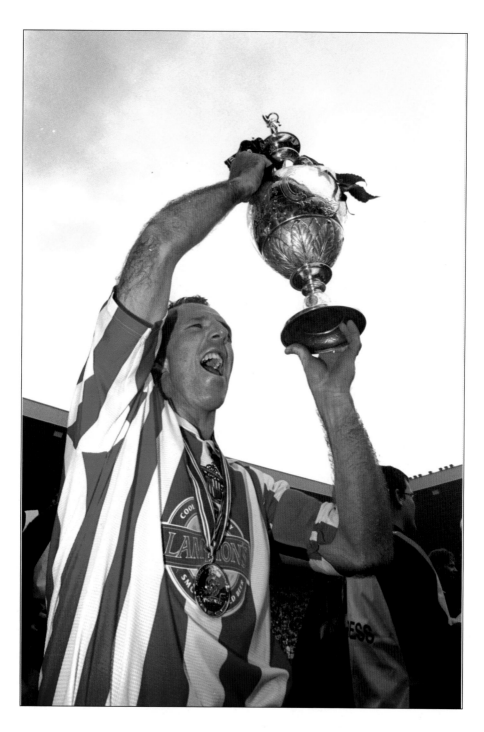

I lifted the Championship trophy twice: at Roker Park in 1996 and here at
the Stadium of Light at the end of the 105 point season in 1999.

Celebrating our equaliser in the 1998 Play-off final with Charlton at Wembley. The match ended 4-4 after extra time before we lost 7-6 on penalties. We re-grouped and came back stronger than ever the following season, winning the League with a record 105 points.

Kevin Phillips broke Brian Clough's post war club goal-scoring record with his 35th goal of the season to put us 2-1 up.

Celebrating my second goal which put us 3-2 ahead.

Sasa Ilic saved Mickey Gray's penalty...

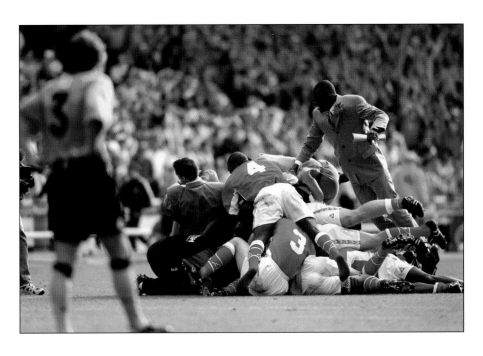

...and Charlton celebrated, but we didn't complain about our lot.
We were the best team in the league that season and the following year
we came back to prove it.

The Red and White Army took defeat on the chin in a sporting manner like ourselves. They were the best in the league too.

I know how great Sunderland can be. That's why I came back.

front we had young Brian Usher and Nicky Sharkey, plus George Mulhall who was really tough and effective on the left and a pair of very skilful inside men in George Herd and Johnny Crossan. It was a very settled side and we steered clear of injuries most of the time, so week in week out we'd be unchanged.

While the Charlton game is my greatest memory, my other greatest days came in the FA Cup. I'd have loved to have played in a Cup Final and we got close a few times with fantastic cup runs in the early 1960s. In 1960/61 we lost out in a quarter-final replay to Tottenham, who that season became the first team of the century to do the 'double.' We had an amazing Cup run. We started off by beating Arsenal in the Third round with a couple of goals from Stan and then we won away to Liverpool in the Fourth round. They were in the Second Division like us then and so were Norwich who we were drawn away to in the Fifth round. That game at Carrow Road was probably my second greatest memory after the Charlton game in which we won promotion.

We had to defend for just about the whole game. We had a strong defence, as I've said, and we were sorely tested that day, but didn't concede a goal. Everyone defended for everything they were worth. I think we only got one corner and it came with about ten minutes left. As usual I went up for it and I met it with as good a header as I've ever connected with. They used to have bits of string in the top corner of each net and when the ball ended up in the top corner of the net it just stayed there! Norwich threw everything at us after that, but we held out.

We'd gone to that match by train and on the way back it was full of Sunderland supporters, so we were up and down the train signing autographs and joining in the celebrations all the way back. Come the Monday and all of the team were sat round the radio listening to the draw and it gave us Tottenham at home. They had Bobby Smith playing centre-forward for them and that was enough for me to think about. He was the hardest centre-forward in the top division and, of course, they were a great team, but we did a great job on them.

We were trailing 1-0, but fought back to draw level. I dived in to head a corner goalwards. They managed to block that one off the line, but they couldn't clear it and Willie McPheat managed to equalise. Willie was a big lad who later broke his leg against Leeds when someone went over the top on him. That was one of the sad things about the game.

After Willie equalised against Spurs we pounded them so much that a player of Danny Blanchflower's calibre had to resort to just kicking the ball into the stand to relieve the pressure. Spurs hung on, though, and walloped us in the replay 5-0 at White Hart Lane where we severely missed Jimmy McNab. I was dying to win the FA Cup, but we never managed it and whenever I see little Bobby Kerr he never forgets to tell me that, while I was the Player of the Century, he won the Cup!

That early sixties Sunderland side was a great team and after we won promotion we should have gone on to be successful. If Alan Brown had stayed we would have been successful, but he left to go to Sheffield Wednesday, who he took to the Cup Final a couple of years later. The club should never have let him go. It was a huge shock to us when he left. Everyone had the greatest of respect for him and it's not often in football that every player has respect for the manager.

Once he left it was chaos. We were going into a first season back at top level and we had no manager. The trainer Arthur Wright did his best for a while, but it was a very dodgy time. Eventually George Hardwick was brought in as manager and he wasn't too bad in his brief time there, but then the Scotsman came, Ian McColl. He was the wrong man for the club. He brought in Jim Baxter, who was the greatest left-footed player I ever saw, but I can say no more about him. McColl then brought in the centre-half George Kinnell who was a mate of Baxter's and suddenly the team started to split up and factionalise.

I was in the reserves, but I never stopped playing. I was a professional and had my pride. A lot of our regular players disappeared to other clubs and I knew the time was getting close when I'd have to leave. When Alan Brown came back to replace McColl it was a very different football club to the one he'd left. He gave me a free transfer which worked out well for me. Nat Lofthouse signed me for Bolton, but I'd have loved to have finished my career at Sunderland.

Sunderland was my club and it always will be. I'd been gone ten years when the fans voted me Sunderland's Player of the Century in the club's Centenary Year. I've become a better player in every year I've not been playing, but I deserved the award in one respect and that is I gave everything for the red and white stripes.

I have now got a new hip and a new knee and I say I left the others at Roker Park and Sunderland is where my heart is too. Today there are some Prima Donnas in the game, but there certainly weren't any when I played and certainly not in our side. That 1964 team was fantastic and that year I was named as runner up to Bobby Moore in the Footballer of the Year

Awards. It was a great honour to finish second to Bobby who was one of England's greatest ever players.

My own international career started by playing against England. I won my first couple of caps with Millwall before I signed for Sunderland after I started to hear rumours that I might get called up by the Republic of Ireland. Ireland were due to meet England at Wembley in a qualifying game for the 1958 World Cup, so I paid to see the game at Wembley and kept my eyes firmly on England's centre-forward who was Manchester United's Tommy Taylor. He scored a hat-trick as England won 5-1 and was obviously an excellent player who would be hard to handle.

My Dad was a real Irishman with a strong Irish accent and he thought I had a chance of playing in the forthcoming game with England at Dalymount Park, but to be honest after seeing Tommy Taylor at Wembley I wasn't in a great rush to play! I was never actually informed by the Irish FA that I was in the squad before, one day, I picked up a newspaper and there was a tiny bit in the corner that said, "Hurley gets first cap v England." As a twenty year-old I was a nervous wreck and as it got closer to the game I decided that the only way I was going to make a name for myself was to make sure that Tommy Taylor didn't score. I wasn't the kind of centre-half to stick to centre-forwards tightly, but on this occasion I stuck to him like glue. When the first cross came over I was up like a bird to head it away and I went on from there. We were winning 1-0 in the last minute when Tom Finney put over a cross. Tommy Taylor ran to the near post and I went with him only for the cross to go over me to the far post where John Atyeo equalised.

We should have won the game rather than drawing, but at least Taylor hadn't scored and according to the papers I was one of the stars of the day. My Dad was working at Ford and said he didn't do any work for the next four weeks because all people wanted to do was talk to him about the game.

Once I came to Sunderland, of course, all people wanted to do all of the time was to talk about football and that was marvellous. To cap it all, after all the wonderful years I had at Roker Park as a player I got the chance to return in 1973 when I was manager of Reading and we were drawn away to Sunderland in the Fourth round of the FA Cup. It seems strange that, after being desperate to win the Cup with Sunderland, fate transpired to somehow involve me in the triumph of 1973. Of course, on the day, I wanted my team to hammer the backsides off them if we could, but after a draw at Sunderland we lost in the replay. I couldn't believe the Cup draw when we were given a tie at Roker, for me it was like a long lost son going back home.

In the build up to the tie I kept telling my players at Reading that they didn't know what it was to be famous until they'd been to Sunderland. When we arrived the players went out to look at the pitch. I hadn't even stepped out at this point and the crowd were already chanting, "Charlie, Charlie." It was brilliant for me. The lads hadn't really believed me, but they came back inside and said, "You'll have to go out and see the fans, boss," and this was still ages before the game.

Our goalkeeper Steve Death, who has since passed away, produced a fantastic performance and we held out for a 1-1 scoreline. In the replay the funny thing was that after we'd lost 3-1, there were Sunderland fans outside the Boardroom chanting for me. Some of the Reading directors were a little concerned that things would get out of hand, so I had to go down and talk to them. There was no problem, of course. Those people at Reading didn't understand. These people were just wanting to show they hadn't forgotten me. I certainly hadn't forgotten them. I've never really left Sunderland and it's never left me.

JIMMY MONTGOMERY
GOALKEEPER 1958–1977 & 1980-1982

BORN 9 October 1943, Sunderland
SIGNED June 1958 as apprentice. Re-signed 7 August 1980
SUNDERLAND CAREER 627 games
HONOURS FA Cup winner 1973, Division Two Championship 1976,
Promotion from Division Two 1963/64, European Cup winner 1979
LEFT Free transfer to Birmingham City, 18 March 1977, Second spell:
retired July 1982

Arguments rage about which was the greatest Wembley goal, but the greatest save seen there is beyond debate. That accolade goes to Jimmy Montgomery for his astonishing 'double' save from Leeds United's Trevor Cherry and Peter Lorimer in the greatest Cup Final upset of all time. Monty made over 150 more appearances for Sunderland than any other player, despite initially leaving when only 33, a young age for a keeper. Jim made spectacular saves on a weekly basis and is a legendary figure to all Sunderland supporters and is synonymous with the club the world over.

Leeds United 0 v Sunderland 1

FA Cup Final
Saturday 5 May 1973

Wembley Stadium
Attendance: 100,000

Monty proves unbeatable as Sunderland take the Cup back to Wearside in the biggest FA Cup final shock ever

Teams

Don Revie	**Managers**	Bob Stokoe
David Harvey	1	Jimmy Montgomery
Paul Reaney	2	Dick Malone
Trevor Cherry	3	Ron Guthrie
Billy Bremner	4	Mickey Horswill
Paul Madeley	5	Dave Watson
Norman Hunter	6	Ritchie Pitt
Peter Lorimer	7	Bobby Kerr
Allan Clarke	8	Billy Hughes
Mick Jones	9	Vic Halom
Johnny Giles	10	Ian Porterfield
Eddie Gray	11	Dennis Tueart
(Sub. Terry Yorath)		
	Scorer	Porterfield 31

Referee: K Burns

EVERYONE REMEMBERS ME for my save in the 1973 FA Cup Final, but if I hadn't made another important one in the Third round away to Notts County, our cup run would have been over before it even started! People often ask why Bob Stokoe made his famous run across to me at the final whistle at Wembley. Bob always said it was a combination of the save at Notts County, a save in the semi-final from George Armstrong and the double save in the final.

I remember the save from Les Bradd at Notts County well because we would have been out of the Cup if I hadn't managed to get to it. We were 1-0 down late in the game. Les had already scored and he had another great chance, but I managed to get to it and a few minutes later Dave Watson equalised with a great header to get us a replay and we went from there.

We beat Reading after a replay and then were drawn away to Manchester City in the Fifth round. They had a great side with people like Colin Bell, Franny Lee, Rodney Marsh and Mickey Summerbee and were favourites for the Cup after knocking out Liverpool, who went on to win the title that year. We played well that day at Maine Road, though, and drew 2-2. I had a lot of saves to make, but managed to toss one in too! But we took them back to Sunderland with over 50,000 there. I keep saying at Talk-ins that the rest of the lads didn't know I was on a crowd bonus!

The replay was a great game. Look at the goals that we scored, fabulous goals. It was a night of electric magic and, if the team were superb, the crowd was unbelievable and we deserved to beat Manchester City. After that we got past Luton in the quarter-final and drew Arsenal in the semi-final at Hillsborough. They were looking to reach the final for the third year running, but we beat them 2-1. The lads played great and we probably could have been more than 1-0 up at half-time. It was in the first half, though, that I had to make an important save right at the foot of my post from George Armstrong. I had to change direction after beginning to dive and it came at an important time in the game.

The build up to the final was a lot of fun. We played golf, pool, snooker, had a laugh and a few bevvies. As we still had three league games left to complete our season, we had a game at Orient as well on the Monday before the Cup Final, but I didn't play in that game and neither did Ian Porterfield. We spent the week at Selsdon Park hotel and had a great time. Everything was nice and relaxed. There was no tension. Bob Stokoe took it off us with dealing with the media, Arthur Cox took it off us with the little games we played and Billy Elliot helped in his own way with his dry humour. They kept us level-headed and we spent the week laughing and joking. It was a perfect scenario, just a fabulous time. We went to the Sports Writers' Dinner – no other Cup Final team had done that and we had a TV crew on the bus on the way to the match. It was the first time that had happened. That was the way it was. We didn't have to think about it. If we had thought about playing that Leeds team, with 11 internationals, one of the best teams in the land, you probably would have frozen up. So Bob, Arthur and Billy just kept us relaxed.

Teams are notorious for freezing at Wembley, but for us the opposite was true. Leeds came out hoping that this Second Division team were going to clam up and there was no way we were going to do that. If anyone was nervous it was them. They were Cup holders, the dominant club side of the era and still faced criticism for not winning enough trophies. All the pressure was on them because of the sheer weight of expectation.

Before the game we had talked about who was going to mark who. Ritchie [Pitt] was going to take care of Allan Clarke, one of the greatest goalscorers of his generation, because before the game we thought if he was tackled hard Clarke might not come back for more. But Mick Jones would keep coming back time after time, so Dave Watson was going to have him. Ritchie says he was fortunate to get the first tackle in and from that first tackle, they knew we were in the game. We didn't give them time to play, it was like when Reidy was at Sunderland, he wouldn't allow other players time on the ball. That's the way we had to do it. Don't give them time.

We were relentless in not giving Giles and co time on the ball. Him and Bremner could thread wonderful passes through and, once we stopped, Johnny Giles they resorted to the long ball. Eddie Gray was supposed to be going to have the beating of Dick Malone, but we had Bobby Kerr doubled up on him. Bobby helped Dick restrict Gray and when we had the ball Maloney was helping Bobby out by overlapping. It was an indication of how we worked as a collective, everybody was tackling and blocking.

Dave Watson was by far the Man of the Match. Unbelievable. A few years ago I went to Sky TV on a programme with Richard Keys. We were sitting, going through the game. It was the third time I'd watched it in full. We were brilliant that day, played superb. Looking at the game their keeper,

David Harvey, actually had more saves to make. Had it been 1-0 to them, David would have been sitting where I was sitting, being the hero. I had to make the double save, but the other saves I had in the game were all comfortable whereas their keeper had more to make, one in particular where he got a vital touch to one Ron Guthrie smacked!

For us it was a whole team effort from the start, but obviously the famous double save I made mid-way through the second half earned me worldwide attention. The ball was played to the right hand side of the box about 35 yards out. Paul Reaney knocked it towards the far post where Trevor Cherry got past Dick Malone and headed back across me. I was going one way and had to start going the other way to reach it, but I managed to palm it out. As I was on the ground I saw the ball go to a white shirt. I used my instinct to get up and make the save. I got my hand to it and pushed it up where it hit the bar. I turned round while I was still on the ground and saw Dick Malone running clear. Nothing comes to mind at the time, you've just got to deal with the next situation. The only thought I had was that I'd got a hand to it. I thought nothing more about it even when Bob Stokoe ran up to me at the final whistle – I didn't know why he did it at the time. It wasn't until we got the Cup and went to the place for interviews and the reporters were going on and on about it that I started to realize how good a save people thought it was.

Being ready to make a second save was something I trained hard for. Sometimes you can do nothing, but get to a ball and parry it into a dangerous area if you can't get it away from goal, so you have to be ready to spring for the follow up. I used to practice pushing myself up off the floor without using my hands because in those situations if you can have both hands with which to try and block the ball it gives you a better chance of making a save. I try to teach that to kids now – if you can dive and get up without using your hands, you have an advantage.

To win the FA Cup with Sunderland was fantastic. After the match I remember everyone getting hold of Bob Cass, who was one of the journalists with us, and throwing him into the bath. That was the beauty back then with the media. We went out together, we got ratted together, but whatever you said to them, nothing went beyond that. You could have a chat and give them your stories. The lads now – I wouldn't have their life.

The Cup Final was a long time ago now, but everyone still talks to me about it. Walking around the town I get it, and I was in hospital recently and someone came up to me and said, "Oh Jim, can you remember that far back?" and I said, "of course I can." I still believe that if Sunderland won the Cup next year, it wouldn't be the same because we're never going to be such vast underdogs again. You are never going to get such a game that we are so much the underdog. Outside of Sunderland it was never expected that we could win because Leeds then were such a terrific side. It's nice – it's how I'll be remembered.

We stayed in the south after the match. The Cup run had meant a few league games had to be re-arranged and we had another two to play on the Monday and Wednesday after Wembley. We played at Cardiff on the Monday. They needed point to stay up and we drew 1-1. I let a penalty in that night. I saved seven out of nine that year, so we weren't too unhappy to draw. Jimmy Scoular was Cardiff's manager. He'd been captain of Newcastle in the 1955 FA Cup Final when Bob Stokoe won there as a player, so everybody was happy. We had a great night out in Cardiff.

We came home on the Tuesday. The bus with our wives on had actually brought the Cup home. Bobby Kerr's wife and mine had sat at the front of the bus with the trophy which must have bemused a few motorists! On the coach home we knew nothing about the parade that was planned for that night. Just before we got to Scotch Corner we started to see Sunderland banners appearing and as we got further north there were more and more of them. It was only when we got to Carrville at Durham that we knew there was an open-topped bus to take us the rest of the way into Sunderland. The number of people who were there all the way into Sunderland and ending up at Roker Park was absolutely incredible.

I played well over 600 games for Sunderland, but the ones I always get asked about are the Cup Final and the cup tie against Manchester United at Roker, where I kicked the ground taking a goal-kick and the ball went to Denis Law, who equalised. I may as well have not played the rest of the games! Obviously the Cup Final was a major highlight, because there's unfortunately been nothing like it since, and before that it had been 1937 since the club won a major trophy, so you can understand why that's one of the occasions which people want to talk about.

I was a young goalkeeper in the Cup quarter-final against Man Utd in 1964, although I'd been in the team for a couple of years. The tie went to three games, although we would have won first replay at Roker Park if I hadn't made that rick, which allowed Law to equalise. In retrospect it was probably a good thing. I got through it. If you can get through that at an early age it can help immensely, I came through that adversity and it helped me through the rest of my career. The crowd were brilliant with me but there was good banter.

In the first game of that tie at Old Trafford we played superbly. Johnny Crossan was magnificent that day and we were winning 3-1 with four minutes left when I was injured and United went on to score two late goals to force a replay. People often say I got up too quickly after being flattened and should have stayed down longer, but that isn't the case. I wouldn't have got up and continued if I didn't think I could. I'd been smacked in the face with a ball from Denis Law. Arthur Wright, our trainer, came on, God Bless him, to give me some treatment. In those days it was just a sponge and that was it. It wasn't all the medics they have now. He took a bit of flak for fixing me up. I felt OK. It was just because from the resulting corner kick, United scored and that was the defining factor. The ball came across and they scored and there was nothing I could have done about. It was just one of those things.

Apart from those two games, there are a lot of others I remember. I think I actually made a better save than the one in the Cup Final in a league game against Hull City, but because there was only about 20,000 there and the match wasn't on TV it's not as famous. It was like Banksy's save against Pelé at the 1970 World Cup. It's like all big occasions – they are remembered at your wake.

There was a game at Charlton in December 1963 where we drew 0-0 and I had a really good game that I remember very well and one at Huddersfield a year earlier, where we were battered for the first half, but eventually won 3-0 with Cloughie scoring two and George Mulhall one.

The team we had at that time was a great team. I have more memories of that 1963/64 side than I have of the 1976 promotion team, maybe because I left a year later. In fact I remember very little of the season where we won the Second Division in '76. In the team that won promotion in 1964 we made very few changes, it was basically the same starting eleven week in week out. If everyone was fit they were in the team.

I was a young lad, but I had experienced players in front of me. There was Charlie Hurley, Len Ashurst and Jim McNab. They looked after you. There was a good mix of the experienced players and the youngsters. We had some young blood up front in Nick Sharkey and Brian Usher, but George Herd and Johnny Crossan could look after them. We had a few lads who could look after themselves such as Johnny Crossan and George

Mulhall, Johnny could be very nasty on the pitch, but off it he was a really nice fella. Then there were people like Len Ashurst, who, for tenacity, couldn't be beaten.

Later on we signed Jim Baxter. The man was a genius. We used to call his left foot 'the claw'. He used to say to the forwards, "you run, and the ball will be there when you get there," and it would be. That's the way he was. We never saw the very best of him at Sunderland. I'd seen him play for Rangers and Scotland and he was even better when he was in his prime.

A year after England won the World Cup Jim famously indulged in a bit of keepy-uppy at Wembley as Scotland beat England 3-2 and claimed to be the true world champions! He wasn't quite so happy when he sat next to me at Wembley the day England actually won the World Cup! There were a load of us at the game and I was sat next to Jim, Neil Martin and George Kinnell – all Scots and they were up when West Germany scored. You can imagine the banter, it was brilliant!

Although I played for England at Under 23 and youth level I never got a full cap. The nearest I got to one was being on the bench at Wembley for an international against France in 1969. Gordon Banks was in goal and barely had a couple of goal-kicks to take as we won 5-0. The funny thing was he'd played for Stoke against us at Roker Park the week before the game and had got injured. He was doubtful for the international, but recovered and was selected. That was the nearest I got. I was in the original party of forty for the 1970 World Cup, but missed out when the squad was whittled down. Alex Stepney and Peter Bonetti went as back up to Banksy. I felt that I should have gone because Stepney wasn't having the best of times at Man United and Bonetti was a little bit in and out. Then again Alex was at Man United, Peter was with Chelsea who had just won the cup and Sunderland had just been relegated.

As things turned out of course, Banksy was unavailable for the quarter-final game and so Bonetti played against West Germany and got blamed for the defeat, but he wasn't a bad keeper. Nowadays people talk about Peter Bonetti and remember him for the West Germany game when things didn't go well for him, but he was an unbelievable keeper on his day. In contrast I'm remembered for the 1973 Cup Final and it's something people can't take away from me. Two careers summed up in one game each. Thankfully mine was when I covered myself in glory!

That was the highlight of my time at Sunderland where I would have loved to have stayed for longer, but I was transferred by Jimmy Adamson during the 1976/77 season. I got on well with big Baz [Barry Siddall], who was a great lad. Bob Stokoe had left with Adamson taking over and I've no idea why he wanted to get rid of me. I never knew why. It must have been a case of a new manager coming in and wanting his own people around him. You move on in football, it's part of how the game works, but I didn't want to.

Jimmy Adamson asked if I would go on loan to Southampton. I played five games for them, but I didn't like the place. You had the Osgoods and Channons there, but it wasn't the place for me. Then I signed for Birmingham on a month's loan. On the last week of the loan Willie Bell said, "I'm going to play you against Derby County." I saved a penalty from Charlie George, we drew 0-0 and I signed for them on the Monday.

Birmingham were scrapping alongside Sunderland for First Division safety and my new club was due to visit my old one late in the season at Roker Park. I said in the paper the night before that it would be great if we could draw 0-0, then Birmingham could stop up and hopefully so would Sunderland. As it turned out Sunderland won 1-0. Afterwards I was upstairs in the bar and Jimmy Adamson came across and said sarcastically, "Well you were nearly right." I just turned away and walked off. It was ironic that at the end of the season Birmingham were safe and Sunderland went down. While I didn't want Sunderland to go down, I was chuffed to bits it went wrong for Adamson because he was such an arrogant man. He did the same to Bobby Kerr as he did to me.

I had a couple of years with Birmingham and then signed for Nottingham Forest. It was a great experience to be involved in the European Cup and to win a medal as sub to Peter Shilton. They were a great set of lads at Forest. Cloughie and Peter Taylor were the best managerial pairing I've ever been under. They knew the players they had. They never bothered about team talks or even tactics as such, it would simply be, "Trevor get the ball. Give it to Robbo," and so on. It was unbelievable, even uncanny. Everyone just knew what he had to do. There were lads there like Martin O'Neill, John McGovern and John O'Hare that were beautifully blended together and they were a great, great side.

I came back to Roker Park in 1980, but didn't play any more first team games. I was coaching the youth team and would like to have stayed, but when Alan Durban came he got rid of me and gave the job to Leighton James. I came back again under Terry Butcher, but when Reidy came he wanted his own man in the job and I left again. That happens in football.

I used to be a regular in the lounge they named the Jimmy Montgomery Suite at Roker Park, but when the move came to the new stadium that ended.

I was sad about leaving Roker Park. Someone said to me, "Forget about the past. We're moving to a new stadium and we're going to start anew." They didn't want to know us for a long time. That's changed now, though, and we former players do a few things for Sunderland.

I still do some coaching at Bradford City twice a week. Former Sunderland keeper Mark Prudhoe was doing it and when he finished there he said for me to give Toddy [Colin Todd] a ring, so I did and I've been there ever since. My daughter lives down that way, so I stay with her and travel on to Bradford. I enjoy it. The odd thing is I've worked with Newcastle for a while as well, but I haven't done any goalkeeping coaching for Sunderland. Maybe one day.

GARY ROWELL
MIDFIELDER/STRIKER 1972–1984

BORN   6 June 1957, Seaham, County Durham
SIGNED   August 1972 as Apprentice
SUNDERLAND CAREER   297 games, 103 goals
HONOURS   Promotion from Division Two 1980
LEFT   Transferred to Norwich, August 1984

From 1977/78 until he left in 1984 Gary Rowell was top scorer every year at Sunderland barring the 1979/80 promotion season, which he largely missed through injury. One of only three players to score over a century of post-war goals for the club, and the only local lad to do so, Gary is idolized by a generation of Sunderland supporters who will never forget the fact that Gary lived the dream of scoring a hat-trick for Sunderland away to Newcastle!

Newcastle United 1 v Sunderland 4

League Division Two
Saturday 24 February 1979

St James' Park.
Attendance 34,733

Rowell hat-trick provides Gary with immortality on Wearside

Teams

Bill McGarry	**Managers**	Billy Elliott
Steve Hardwick	1	Barry Siddall
John Brownlie	2	Mick Henderson
Irving Nattrass	3	Joe Bolton
Mick Martin	4	Kevin Arnott
		(Sub. Mick Docherty)
John Bird	5	Jeff Clarke
John Blackley	6	Shaun Elliott
Alan Shoulder	7	Gordon Chisholm
Nigel Walker	8	Wilf Rostron
Peter Withe	9	Wayne Entwistle
Terry Hibbitt	10	Bob Lee
John Connolly	11	Gary Rowell
Connolly 50	**Scorers**	Rowell 6, 26,pen 62, Entwistle 72

Referee: P Patridge

IF SOMEONE ASKED if you could score a hat-trick, and granted you a wish to score it against any team you wanted, a hundred out of a hundred Sunderland fans would say they'd love to score it against Newcastle. I was fortunate enough to be able to do that. Whether it would have been better at Roker Park or St. James's I'm not sure. I would have loved to have scored a hat-trick against Newcastle at Roker Park. But in a way it's even better the way it turned out, because, to have scored it at Newcastle, you're in enemy territory. That made me, in the eyes of the fans.

Since the Second World War only Kevin Phillips, Len Shackleton and myself have scored over one hundred goals for Sunderland, but to be honest in some ways my other goals, including my home hat-trick against Arsenal, almost pale into insignificance compared to my hat-trick in the derby.

Going into the game we were pushing for promotion. It was late February and we'd been unbeaten since before Christmas, although we had drawn too many games. We had a settled side that included some terrific players like Joe Bolton, who was as hard as nails at left-back, Barry Siddall in goal, who, like Joe, was a real character, and in the centre of defence Jeff Clarke and Shaun Elliott were superb. I'd been in the team a little longer than Shaun, but when he and Kevin Arnott made their debut together a couple of years earlier the three of us all did well. Kevin was a great passer of the ball and he would set one of my goals up against the Mags.

I always think, though, that no matter what position you are in the league – the derby is the biggest game ever. As a kid I had no other ambition other than to play for Sunderland. That was the be all and end all of my ambition. Once you do that – and it doesn't happen overnight because you have to work your way through the youth team and the reserves – eventually if you do make it, then the game you want to play in is the derby. Pulling a red and white shirt on for the Newcastle game is biggest thing you can ever do. It's fantastic. I can never understand people who say it's just another game, because it just so isn't. That's a ridiculous thing to say because they just devalue it. This is one of the biggest derbies in the world. You've got the Milan derby, Real Madrid v Barcelona, Celtic v Rangers – but these teams play each other when they're going for the league titles. Can you imagine Sunderland and Newcastle playing each other for the

Premiership or in a Cup Final? They usually meet each other when one or the other is struggling. Can you imagine what it would be like if they were both flying. As big as the fixture is now, can you imagine what it would be like if both were in top four? You have to go back to the early fifties for that scenario. That is my background. I'm steeped in red and white. I used to go to Sunderland games. I was a fanatical Sunderland supporter and I still am. I don't want any extra credit for that – it's just the way I am.

For that particular derby game we set off from Roker Park. You always get a hundred or so people seeing you off, you know, the ones who can't get tickets for the game, but want to come and urge you on as you set off. That's something I loved as well. It's not just the ninety minutes on derby day, it's the build up, it was getting on the bus and going past the Blue Bell in Fulwell with everybody there in red and white. Then, as you go north, you start to see a mixture of red and white and black and white. By the time you get to the Tyne Bridge, it's all black and white. All that is part of the derby day experience for me.

My game was in the Second Division, but it still mattered more than any other because it was the derby match. You get to St. James's and you get abuse from their fans – but it's great, I wouldn't have it any other way. Even the bus journey is special. I can remember I used to get dead excited just being on the bus!

You've got the build-up to a derby match and then the work starts. The worst bit is the hour before game because you're stuck in the dressing room and you just want to get out there. I don't believe people who say they don't get nervous before a derby game. Before any top level game, you should be geared up – but for a derby game you should be even more so.

Once the match kicked off we got off to a great start. I scored the first goal, which was very scrappy. Gordon Chisholm headed on Jeff Clarke's free-kick and Wilfie Rostron got another touch to knock it on to me – I lunged at it, and it ended up in the net. It really settled everyone down. An early goal for Sunderland was perfect. It was like nothing else. Fantastic. A goal for Sunderland is a goal – you work all week for it. Scoring it in a derby – there's nothing better. As a kid it's what everybody dreams of. You score that goal and you're living out your mates' dreams. I was as chuffed as it's possible to be, but I had to keep my concentration as we all did because it is well known in football that you are never as vulnerable as when you've just scored. If you let it go to your heads you end up giving a goal away and then it's the opposition with their tails up.

They put us under a bit of pressure, and we broke away and got a second goal, which put us right in the driving seat. I was playing behind the front two. Usually away from home I'd take on more of a midfield role, while at home I'd play more up front, depending on the game. A lot of people think I was an out-and-out striker because I scored a hundred goals, but a lot of the time I was in midfield and that suited me because very often I could time a run into the box without being picked up.

That day I was anticipating being more in midfield, but because we'd had such a good start, I found myself supplementing the front two more and more.

Kevin Arnott picked me out with a great through ball for the second goal. I'd played with Kev for years and years – we played together as kids, so we had a good understanding of each other's game. I'd make runs and he'd pick me out. So Kev put the ball right in front of me. 2-0 up. Brilliant. The fans went really quiet apart from in the Sunderland end. From then until half-time the Mags were really quiet. We could have even had another goal, but the referee disallowed an effort from Bob Lee to bring play back for a free-kick to us!

After I'd scored the second believe it or not I really wasn't thinking about the possibility of a hat-trick. You're still part of a team. You still have a job to do. You can't be too insular. It's more important to win the game. A couple of years earlier I'd played in a derby game where we were 2-0 up and they came back to draw 2-2, so I'd learned from that not to get too far ahead of myself.

We went in at half-time, and it was a great feeling. Billy Elliott, who was our long term caretaker-manager at the time, said, "Don't let them in, don't give them a goal and let them back in the game." But we did! John Connolly scored and you just began to wonder if it was going to slip away from us again.

Anyway, we were under pressure for a bit, and I went back into midfield. The crucial moment was when we broke away and got a penalty when Micky Henderson was brought down by Kenny Mitchell. Ironically, Kenny was a Sunderland lad.

Of course I was the penalty taker and I had a reputation for being cool and slotting them in. It was probably the most pressured penalty I ever took in my life when I think about it. I knew if I missed they'd get a massive psychological boost, and they could go on and at least draw the game, because psychology in football is everything. But I knew if I scored – more than it being a hat-trick penalty – I knew if I scored the game was over.

Suddenly they'd had their spell, but we've scored as I side-footed my penalty to Steve Hardwick's left and recreated the two-goal lead. A lot of people say that I looked really cool taking that penalty, but I was anything but. My stomach was really churning. I just remember looking up as I waited to take the kick and wishing it was in front of the Sunderland fans, but I was in front of the Newcastle fans. Of course, there was all the whistling and booing and the goal was shrinking before my eyes. Maybe there was extra pressure on me because I had a very good penalty record, so people expected me to score. To be honest there was enough pressure on me already knowing that if I scored we'd won the game, because they weren't going to come back from 3-1 behind. I thought, "If I miss it the place will go up and I'll be responsible." The pressure was on and I was feeling it – I'm not ashamed to admit it.

I held my nerve and put it in. The feeling was one of relief and it wasn't until I was running back to the half-way line that I realised I'd scored a hat-trick at St. James's Park. The penalty was the key moment in the game. It was such a relief for it to go in. Looking back I'm actually pleased it was in front of the Newcastle fans because I'd really stuck one up them. For a Sunderland lad it doesn't get much better than that.

As we were running back we were looking at the Sunderland fans and they were jumping all over. They knew we'd won the game, we knew we'd won the game – there was just no way that Newcastle were coming back into it. Most importantly they knew they weren't getting back into it. But then, to make it even better for us, we got a fourth – and at that point there was still a fair bit to go in the game.

I nearly scored the fourth goal. Somebody played it to me – I knew exactly what I wanted to do, I wanted to get to the byline and hang it up at the far post, that's very difficult to defend. As it happened my cross could well have drifted in. Wayne Entwistle was playing up front for us and he did what anyone would have done, and rightly so – he got to it and just buried it. That gave me as much of a buzz as anything. I'd scored a hat-trick and set one up for Wayne for good measure!

We were 4-1 up with about 20 minutes remaining for us to coast through the game. It doesn't get any better. There we were, on their patch, bossing the game. They were completely demoralized, which gave us as big a buzz as winning because they're our biggest rivals. Newcastle were down and out and we were playing with them in many ways.

I don't mind admitting that we lorded it a bit to the point that, with about ten minutes to go, when we got a free-kick, me, Kev Arnott and

Wilfie Rostron were just laughing. We were thinking, "Do we go for a fifth or do we take the piss?" This was in a derby game, and I've never had that kind of feeling before or since! It was that good. We ended up having a shot that came to nothing, but, for the closing stages of the match, really we were just toying with them. The pressure was off us to that much of an extent that we were just laughing – thinking, "this is fantastic!"

The game finished. I looked round and the place was empty. The Mags had gone in their droves, the Sunderland fans were celebrating. As moments go they don't come any better. You've gone and done a job, and you've done it better than expected. Fantastic, the sense of elation was incredible and the scenes in the dressing room were as if we'd won the Cup.

Our caretaker-manager Billy Elliott was great. I love Billy – he's a legend. He played for England. He was a trainer when Sunderland won the FA Cup in 1973. He's been around Sunderland for a long, long time and I have loads of respect for him. He was delighted. He was always great with me. I have a lot to thank Billy for. I remember after the game, it wasn't like now – Press Officers didn't exist then. In one of my last in a long line of interviews, someone said to me, "Gary, would it be fair to say, that this means more to you because you hate Newcastle?" and I said, "yeah." I didn't actually say the words, "I hate Newcastle", I just said, "yeah", but in some of the morning papers it was plastered all over the pages. It's true, but it might not be the wisest thing I've ever done, saying it in public, although actually, I just agreed with someone.

Ken Knighton, our coach, came to me the next day – we were in training – he said, "the Gaffer wants to see you in his office." I went in and explained what had happened in a round-a-bout way. I asked, "Am I in trouble?" Billy said, "No, I ******* love it! I think it's great. Get out and finish your training." Billy was red and white to the core, but I was really worried when I walked into his office. I was wondering if the FA had said something about all the furore, but I felt even better when I came out. Billy was brilliant.

He'd been caretaker-manager from just before Christmas. Jimmy Adamson had left to go to Leeds, after which Dave Merrington was care-taker for a couple of months. When he joined Adamson at Leeds, Billy got the job. He didn't have the greatest of starts, in fact the Newcastle game was only the second one we'd won in his first eight league games, but we won six of the next seven and, before the end of the season, topped the table, although we just missed out on promotion at the death. The Board appointed

Ken Knighton from the coaching staff to become manager despite a fans' petition to get Billy the job full-time. As it was, though, we won promotion the next year, so Ken did well.

I can't remember how I celebrated that night after my hat-trick at St. James's Park, so it must have been good! Maybe someone can tell me. Typically we got beat 3-0 at Roker Park by Burnley on the Monday night in an FA Cup replay. I think we must have been hung over from the Newcastle game!

Even now, when I go to games as a summariser on Magic 1152, I hear the fans chanting my name. They have that, "We all live in a Gary Rowell World" song. There's a few other clubs adopted the words, but at Sunderland they've been singing it since I was playing and that's a long time! It is amazing because SAFC v NUFC is real history. To a club like Sunderland, history and tradition is massive. I was raised on stories of Raich Carter and Shack and they're iconic figures to me.

Not long ago I was in the function suite at Stadium of Light for a Sporting Dinner. I passed this table of lads that looked about 19 or 20 years-old. They were good lads, all dressed smartly in their bow ties. One guy came up to me and asked if I had the time would I come over to the table later because they'd all love to meet me and talk to me. I came back and they said, "All we want to know is – what was it like to score a hat-trick against the Mags?" So I gave them chapter and verse. They were great lads. Heart and soul red and white. Some of them may have been one or two at the time of the game. They'd heard about it, though, and wanted to know what it was like. Each one shook my hand and said, "thanks". It made my night. Things like that are fantastic.

I'm a big fan of Monty and Bobby Kerr and I'm in awe of them or anybody to do with the 1973 Cup run. Whenever I'm with Micky Horswill, I'll always steer the conversation to the Man City game when Micky was fantastic. Anything to do with the Cup run and I'm enthralled. After all the '73 lads achieved something that no other Sunderland team has done since the 1930s. For me it's still a thrill when-ever I see Monty or Charlie [Hurley]. Although Charlie wasn't in the '73 team, it's still a buzz as he was such a legend. For people to treat me like that – put me on that same pedastel – is a bit weird. Sometimes I can't quite get my head around it.

GARY BENNETT
CENTRE-HALF 1984-1995

BORN   4 December 1961, Manchester
SIGNED   July 1984 from Cardiff City; £65,000 + £20,000 after 20 games
SUNDERLAND CAREER   443 games, 25 goals
HONOURS   Promotion from Division Two, 1989/90, Division Three
Championship 1987/88, FA Cup Finalist 1992, League Cup Finalist 1985
LEFT   Free transfer to Carlisle United, November 1995

'Benno' was Sunderland's captain of the late 1980s and early 1990s and played
at Wembley in the 1985 League Cup Final, the 1988 League Centenary tournament, the 1990 Play-off Final and the 1992 FA Cup Final. He was a colossus at
centre-back, hard as nails and relished clashes with the games fiercest forwards.
There was more than just brawn to 'Benno's' game though, his trademark was
to slalom forward, his mazy dribbles turning defence into attack. One of his
most dramatic goals changed the course of this crucial game, which Gary selects
as the 'Match of his Life' despite its ultimately disappointing outcome.

Sunderland 4 v Gillingham 3 (after extra time; aggregate 6-6)

Gillingham win on away goals

Division Two/Three Play-off semi-final second leg
Sunday 17 May 1987

Roker Park
Attendance 25,470

Benno's majestic last minute header forces extra-time,
but the Lads still go down

Teams

	Managers	
Bob Stokoe	**Managers**	Keith Peacock
Iain Hesford	1	Phil Kite
Paul Lemon	2	Phil Haylock
Alan Kennedy	3	Graham Pearce
(Sub. David Corner)		
Steve Doyle	4	Les Berry
Frank Gray	5	Trevor Quow
Gary Bennett	6	Colin Greenall
Gordon Armstrong	7	Howard Pritchard
Mark Proctor	8	Mark Weatherley
Keith Bertschin	9	David Smith
Dave Swindlehurst	10	Karl Elsey
Eric Gates	11	Tony Cascarino

	Scorers	
Gates 17, 22	**Scorers**	Pritchard 3
Bennett 88, Bertschin 110		Cascarino 52, 93

Referee: M Peck

I WAS IN THE third of my twelve seasons at Sunderland when this game took place. I'd signed for Len Ashurst, who had been my manager at Cardiff, and then I played for Lawrie McMenemy. We were in a lot of trouble when he left and then Bob Stokoe came in which was tremendous, because obviously he was very highly regarded by Sunderland supporters. He came in for the last seven league games of the 1986/87 season. The situation was that the club was struggling to keep its Second Division status. Sunderland had never been in the Third Division. We were obviously battling to stay up – and to cap it all, these new things called the play-offs came.

When you talk about play-offs, people only think of the play-offs as being the top three or four teams that battle it out for promotion as it is now and has been for some time, but when the play-offs first came in it, was about the third bottom team from the old Second Division fighting for survival. That team met the team who had finished fifth in the league below with the winners of that playing the winners of the play-off between the teams that had finished third and fourth. That situation was new to us and so was the pressure going into it.

Bob Stokoe was a great guy, sort of like Bobby Robson – not the best with names. He got me and Gordon Armstrong mixed up and it's not as if we look like each other at all! He called me Gordon Bennett, but you just accepted him. He was a tremendous fellow, but maybe he came in a little bit too late in the season. He lifted the spirits of the players and tried to keep it simple. It was great to play under him. Right throughout my career I've heard loads of stories about Bob Stokoe and to be managed by him for nine games in all was a privilege.

When Lawrie Mac arrived everybody thought, "He's the new Messiah. He's going to take us back to where to we belong." There was a big hoo-hah at the time because of the wages he was getting paid, which I think were around £100,000. That was huge money especially for the north east at a time when the pits getting shut down and there was a lot of unemployment. I remember that his wages were even talked about in the House of Commons. Lawrie came in and I remember the first five games of that season, we didn't win a game, didn't even score a goal before we played Grimsby. We drew 3-3 and it was like we had won the Cup – we actually scored our first goal and got our first point on the table. We thought that was it and from then on we'd be flying.

Leading up to that season he'd brought in the likes of Eric Gates, David Swindlehurst, Frank Gray, Alan Kennedy and George Burley. He surrounded himself with experienced international pros – like he had at Southampton. He obviously thought, "If I get these players in then that will ease the pressure and they'll be able to take the club on."

I've heard it said that there were cliques at the club at the time, but I don't think there were cliques at all. I think coming up to the north east it's a different ball game for some players. In Sunderland, football is life or death. It's talked about all the time and you usually do find that one or two players that come to the north east – not just Sunderland, but Newcastle and Middlesbrough as well – find it hard to settle because of the pressure to be successful. I think David Swindlehurst for instance found that, especially from the point of view of the north-south divide. He came up and the pressure was on to score the goals, and because we weren't scoring then people were getting picked out. I'll always remember Lawrie Mac saying to Dave, "Well if you can't handle coming up here then come up on a Thursday, train on a Friday, play the game on Saturday and go back home." Dave had two kids down in London and he was up and down on the train all the time, which was tough for him and it was difficult for him to settle. He wanted to get home as quickly as possible because it was affecting his football.

It wasn't just him – the likes of Eric Gates, whose first season at Sunderland was a nightmare, had it tough as well. The following season he was Player of the Year, he turned it around. Alan Kennedy and George Burley found it hard. Dropping down a level they found it hard to find their feet.

Those two had played in and won European finals and suddenly they were in a play-off to decide whether or not we went down into the Third Division. It was a different type of big game to what they were used to and a different type of football and a different type of pressure. No time and space on the ball, because players are in your face, there's hustle and bustle and you don't have time to play the ball in – it's the sort of football where you play it up to the big man as quickly as possible and pick the pieces up. So one or two players did find it difficult to settle and it reflected on the rest of the team.

We had a chance to save ourselves in the last game of the regular season if we beat Barnsley at home. We should have done so, because we were 2-0 up, and then got a penalty. But we missed it and ended up losing 3-2. The confidence in the team drained out when the penalty was missed and obviously Barnsley gained confidence and went on to win the game. Jim Dobbin scored a world class goal for them, which summed up that season – everything went in against us. We came off the pitch that day hoping that Shrewsbury had lost; they had to win to go above us. News drifted in that they had got the win which sent us into the play-offs, where we came up against Gillingham, who'd finished fifth in the Third Division.

It was a shock to system – all of a sudden Sunderland were going to play in the play-offs against Gillingham. We'd never played there before. We were thinking we were going to win. Gillingham had finished fifth in the Third Division. We should have been good enough to beat them especially over two legs, but we went down there for the first leg where we came across big Tony Cascarino, who did a lot of damage. He went on to have a great career, of course, but it was really that Play-off tussle with us that made his name. He scored five goals in the two games, starting with a hat-trick in the first leg in their 3-2 win.

We were in front at half-time in that match after Mark Proctor scored from the spot, but Cascarino equalised with an overhead kick just after half-time and then two mistakes by our goalkeeper Iain Hesford in dealing with David Smith crosses gave Cascarino the chance to score twice more. Straight after they went 3-1 up, though, Proctor pulled one back with a great shot and at 3-2 we still thought we were in with a great shout at Roker Park for the second leg.

There was a lot of pressure because everyone was expecting us to win. We were stunned really by the whole situation let alone the first leg defeat. Everybody was struggling – not just those I've mentioned. Confidence was low throughout the team and that reflected in our performance. After the game we sat down and had a discussion. We were disappointed in how we'd done, but we all thought we had a good chance at Roker Park.

I'd taken a knock in the first leg and was a doubt right up to kick-off, but nothing was going to stop me playing, especially as our other first choice centre-half Steve Hetzke had been forced off at half time in the first leg with substitute Eric Gates coming on for him.

The second leg started badly, though, when Howard Pritchard scored for them in the first few minutes to put us 4-2 down on aggregate. The pressure was back on us and we couldn't find our feet. It was a game where the lead changed hands more than once, though, and mid way through the half Eric Gates scored twice in four minutes to make it 2-1 to us on the day and 4-4 on aggregate. At that point with home advantage we were confident of going on to win.

We should have had a penalty when I was fouled, but nothing was given for that. Then, just past the half hour, we did get a penalty and had we scored it I think we'd have gone on to survive. But it was like the Barnsley game in that Proctor missed and the opposition got a lift. Phil Kite saved Proccy's penalty with his legs. It was a crucial moment.

The score stayed at 4-4 on aggregate until seven minutes into the second half when Gillingham got their own penalty. Iain Hesford did fantastically well to save Colin Greenall's kick, but Trevor Quow got the ball straight back into the danger area and Cascarino made it 2-2 on the day and restored Gillingham's advantage on aggregate.

We thought we still had enough to go on and win the game and, to try something different, I swapped positions with Dave Swindlehurst. Swinders went back to play centre-half and I went up front and managed to score the goal to send us into extra-time. A cross came in and I managed to get my head to it. It was a fair distance out. Everything just fell into place, there was uproar when it hit the net and knowing what the goal meant made it really special as well. To score a goal like that is something you dream about and it came true. It was amazing. You speak to supporters now and they'll tell you. "I was on the way out!" People had thought, "That was it, we're down." There were only a couple of minutes to go when I scored, so it was the last roll of dice really. After I'd scored I was thinking, "Is this it? Can we go on and win and survive?" But it didn't go that way.

The 90 minutes were up almost straight after my goal. The aggregate score was 5-5, each team having won 3-2 on their home ground. The Play-offs were new to everybody, no-one was familiar with them and we didn't know what was happening.

I remember going into it thinking, "Do away goals count?" Nobody knew at the time and, although at that point it made no difference as each leg had ended with the same scoreline, there was the extra-time to think about and would away goals count then? Nobody knew what the outcome would be – I don't even think the referee knew either – and we thought, "Is it going to penalties or what?" We went into extra-time and I remember we had some Newcastle supporters in the Clock Stand Paddock. They had bought tickets to come and cheer the opposition on and there was hell on with them and the Sunderland supporters with quite a few arrests.

As we had done at the beginning of the game we conceded a goal early in extra-time. This time it was Cascarino – again. It was his fifth goal of the Play-off and his 30th of the season. It meant we had to score twice to win because now an aggregate draw would mean we lost on away goals. We did score again, through Keith Bertschin, to make it 4-3 to us on the day and 6-6 on aggregate, but we still needed another goal.

One or two of the lads had picked up injuries during the game – I think we actually finished with ten men. People had pulled hamstrings or calf muscles and they couldn't finish. They just tried to get through it and stretched every sinew to get that goal which would keep us in the division, but obviously we couldn't get it. We threw everything at it, but it just wouldn't happen. You speak to a lot of supporters and they can't remember the actual score. There were so many goals and it was such an entertaining game, but we ended up going down on away goals because the extra-time had been played on our ground! Soon after that the League decided that it was a ridiculous situation for extra-time to count in a two-legged tie where that extra period was only played on one ground giving one side an extra half hour to score an away goal. It was too late to save us, though.

Obviously we were all devastated afterwards. For a club like Sunderland with its tradition and support to be in the Third Division was terrible, but you look back, and Denis Smith came in and the rest is history. We bounced straight back by winning the league a year later and two years further on we were back in the top flight. The signing of Marco Gabbiadini gave Eric Gates a new lease of life and they destroyed teams time and time again, while players like Iain Hesford, who had endured a bad time in the relegation year, showed the character to come back and do well.

Although I've picked out one of the most disappointing days in the club's history as the 'Match of My Life' because that Gillingham game was so crucial, I also had lots of great times at Sunderland and in a way you have to endure the lows to fully appreciate the highs.

My Sunderland career got off to a great start and I never looked back. I scored past the England keeper Peter Shilton in the second minute of my debut in a game we went on to win, so I certainly got off to a good start and the crowd took to me straight away. All of a sudden there's this lad who's playing centre-half and the Sunderland supporters would be thinking, "Oh my God, he's gone missing. What's he doing running up pitch with the ball?"

They'd not seen this for a long time from the centre-half and I was known for going on these runs up the field and the supporters related to it. That was great and scoring one or two vital goals, such as a last minute winner against Manchester United, was a dream come true – especially being a Manchester lad! On that occasion I was upfield in the last minute with the score at 1-1 when the ball came to me. These days if a centre-back is forward in the last minute it's because you are chasing the game, you wouldn't expect centre-backs to be committed up front now if the scores were level late on, but this was a different era and we really wanted to win the game.

I remember Gary Pallister was facing me. He was a great lad, who had just gone to Manchester United from Middlesbrough for a big money fee. I could see him over my shoulder, so I just hooked the ball over his head and he fell for it. I made a good connection on the ball and it flew past the goalkeeper. To score in the last minute like that is comic book boyhood stuff really.

These are the games you dream about playing in. You want to play at the top level, you want to play against the Man Uniteds and Liverpools, Arsenals etc and if you are a Sunderland player you want to play against Newcastle, that's what you dream about being involved in.

I grew up as a Manchester City supporter, but this was 30 to 40 years ago. In those days if City were playing at home, you'd go to see them, but if they were playing away and United were playing at home, you'd go to see United. I was a City supporter, but I went to both clubs. A lot of people did that. If you speak to a lot of Sunderland supporters they'll say, "yeah, we used to watch Sunderland play one week, and then Newcastle the next." It wasn't a problem. You can't do that now though. There'd be chaos.

One of my other big days as a Sunderland player came at Man City. As with the Gillingham game I scored, but we still went down. We took 15,000 supporters to Maine Road even though we were fighting for survival – we had to get a result against Man City. Niall Quinn played up front for City in that game. He scored two and was a real handful. He was a good player. Again we thought we could go and get a result. But we never do anything the easy way at Sunderland and we lost 3-2.

We played really good football in that 1990/91 season and received a lot of plaudits as well. We got relegated, but played entertaining stuff. A prime example was when we played Spurs away and were 2-0 up. They brought on a substitute, I think it was Walsh that came on. We probably should have started shutting up shop – but we continued going forward. We were entertaining, but we lost 3-2 in the end.

There was never a dull game and again, against City we played some smashing stuff. I remember Marco Gabbiadini scored a fantastic goal. A great cross came in and Marco scored a tremendous header. And that was how we were. Denis Smith had us playing entertaining stuff. We kept going forward, we weren't negative. At the final whistle the results started filtering through and we knew we were relegated. Even the Man City supporters applauded us. They couldn't believe it that we'd brought 15,000 supporters and we were going down. They were tremendous – they applauded our supporters, applauded our players and we went across and applauded our supporters. It was one of those days when Sunderland supporters proved yet again that they are in a different class.

Sunderland fans love to see someone getting stuck in, so I had no problems there because I was well known for doing that – even if sometimes I got carried away a bit! The day everyone talks about, of course, is when I got sent off for fighting with David Speedie and he ended up in the Clock Stand Paddock. It was televised too. Everyone all over the country saw it and must have been wondering why I did that. Speedie was a good footballer, but he wasn't well-liked. He was a handful, niggly. He was like a Dennis Wise of his age. Going back a few years we'd had a few run-ins with him particularly in the 1985 League Cup semi-final when he was with Chelsea. He was playing for Coventry when we drew them in the League Cup in 1990, so that gave me the chance to meet him again. I was battling all week to be fit for that game, I was strapped up and he went over the top on me – I reacted like a Sunday league player would and lost the plot a little bit and pushed him into the Clock Stand. The supporters in the Clock Stand kept pushing him out, so I kept pushing him back in saying, "go on, finish him off." Unfortunately they didn't and I got my marching orders. Kevin Ball and I have been sent off five times each for Sunderland, more than anybody else. It's not a record to be proud of, but Kevin would say the same thing, it hurt when you were losing and sometimes it got the better of you. You try to do something about it on the pitch and you get caught out and get marching orders. But I wouldn't change, it was how I played and it's how I would play now. Running out for Sunderland wearing red and white you've got know what it means, not just for yourself, but to the supporters as well. I think if you give 100 per cent, even if you've not the best ability, they can appreciate that.

I wasn't Sunderland's first black player, but with respect to Roly Gregoire, who can claim that achievement, I was the first black player the crowd really took to. These days I do a lot of work for the Show Racism the Red Card campaign. I hope I led by example at Sunderland. Wearside fans got behind me. European teams are 20 years behind us, we've seen players such as Emile Heskey going to play against European teams and getting grief from people because of the colour of his skin.

Looking back I was one of the first black players to play in the north east and hopefully that opened doors for the likes of people who've gone on to play for Middlesbrough and Newcastle as well as Sunderland. You look at the three teams back then and none of them had black players. I think I was the first black captain and the first black captain of any club at Wembley, which is another huge achievement. It's gone on from there. So when I see more and more black players in the north east I do like to think that I helped open those doors for them to come up and say there's no problem with racism up here, because sometimes people get this negative feeling about the north east as being a place that's racist and it's not. I think we've seen that now – even at Sunderland, Middlesbrough and Newcastle Universities – it's a lot more multi-cultural with more people coming into area. Hopefully I played my part in that.

I'm in shock sometimes when people relate to me as a legend at Sunderland. George Best and Pelé and people like that are legends. When people ask how many games you've played – you don't actually realise how many until your career comes to an end, but I know that only four people have played more games for Sunderland than I did and I'm proud of that.

My brother Dave played over 300 games for half a dozen clubs and he was surprised about how closely I've become connected to Sunderland. He's often talking to various people and if they're from the north east, he'll mention me and he can't believe the reaction he gets. A friend of mine rang me recently, he was sat in the pub with a guy talking about me, and he put this guy on the phone and he was going, "No, I don't believe it. I don't believe you're Gary Bennett." I had to prove that I was Gary Bennett! Even at my son's Christening in Wingate in a pub called the Fir Tree, the landlord knew who I was. He came down with his shirts which I signed for him. They wanted pictures taken, they were in shock. It was unbelievable really.

I showed my son a video of some of the goals I'd scored and he was in shock as well. It's hard to take for him, because people are asking now him for his autograph as well. Grown men are telling my little boy what I did. It's funny for my wife as well. I'd like to go shopping to Morrison's and things, but if I go we never get the job done as I'm stopped all of the time. I couldn't watch my lads Leon and Lee play football because people were more interested in me, and it was putting pressure on them because of who their Dad was, people wanted to kick them and it was taking the shine off it for them. That side is sometimes difficult, but that's football and, nice as it is, you take it with a pinch of salt really.

MARCO GABBIADINI
FORWARD 1987-1991

BORN   20 January 1968, Nottingham
SIGNED   22 September 1987, from York City £80,000
SUNDERLAND CAREER   185 games 87 goals
HONOURS   Promotion from Division Two, 1989/90, Division Three
Championship 1987/88, 1 England B cap, 2 under-21 caps
LEFT   Transferred to Crystal Palace, 26 September 1991; £1,800,000

Marco Gabbiadini was such an exciting footballer at Sunderland. He was the most thrilling sight in full flight for Sunderland fans since Dennis Tueart in his heyday. Marco formed a seemingly almost telepathic understanding with Eric Gates, who enjoyed an Indian summer in tandem with Marco. They became renowned as the 'G Force' and left Newcastle in tatters after destroying them in the Play-offs, one of the most important clashes ever played between the old rivals. Marco averaged very nearly a goal every two games in his four years on Wearside, where he became the undoubted hero of the generation of fans who grew up with him.

Newcastle United 0 v Sunderland 2

Division Two Play-off semi-final second leg
Monday 16 May 1990

St James' Park
Attendance: 32,216

The 'G Force' destroy Newcastle on a night when even a pitch invasion couldn't stop Sunderland

Teams

Jim Smith	Managers	Denis Smith
John Burridge	1	Tony Norman
Kevin Scott	2	John Kay
Mark Stimson	3	Reuben Agboola
Roy Aitken	4	Gary Bennett
John Anderson	5	John MacPhail
Darren Bradshaw	6	Gary Owers
(Sub. Kevin Dillon)		
Kevin Brock	7	Paul Bracewell
Billy Askew	8	Gordon Armstrong
(Sub. Liam O'Brien)		
Micky Quinn	9	Eric Gates
Mark McGhee	10	Marco Gabbiadini
Bjorn Kristensen	11	Warren Hawke

Scorers   Gates 13, Gabbiadini 85

Referee: G Courtney

AT THE TIME OF the Play-offs with Newcastle we were a young side. I was a fairly young player myself, so it was the biggest game I'd ever played in – notwithstanding it was against our biggest local rival. The history and passion involved in that fixture, whether it is League or Cup is immense, so to be playing with the potential prize of a place in the top flight at stake made it even more important.

That season we'd already played them twice in the league and in the first leg of the Play-off which had been a very tense goalless affair. All three games had ended up draws, but the second leg of the Play-off semi-final was going to be a case of all or nothing. A place in the Wembley final beckoned.

My first game at St James's Park had been the league visit that season. I'd scored and I can remember the moment that the ball went in the back of the net was the quietest of the game. It was really windy and because of the direction of the wind, it carried the sound away from where we were. Our fans were up at the other end from where I scored. When it went in I was screaming, but I couldn't hear the reaction of our supporters for about two seconds, which is a strangely long time in those circumstances.

The league games against Newcastle that season were special enough because the clubs had only met in one league season in the last decade, Sunderland's relegation season of 1984/85. All that time without hardly a derby match meant when they finally came along, the games had extra intensity; and now here we were playing the Mags for the chance of going back up to the top flight.

Newcastle had had an outstanding season. They were a big side, very experienced with the likes of Roy Aitken, who had joined earlier in the season from Celtic, the irrepressible Micky Quinn partnering Mark McGhee up front and a very underrated player in Kevin Brock running things in midfield. They clearly believed they were going to go up. I think they'd been near the top two for most of the season, while we were fairly middling in what was only our second season after promotion from the Third Division. I can remember late season games against Portsmouth and Wolves that were important for us. By the end of that season we had developed a stubbornness. We wanted to see things through and were in with a chance of making the play-offs with about a dozen games left and knew we had to get results, so we stuck at it. On one away trip down south we went to see Alan Ball in his pub where he showed me his World Cup winner's medal. It was a highlight for me as a young lad to see it.

We'd had some good results away from home that season, including a good 1-1 draw at their place and so going to St. James's Park for the second leg of the Play-offs all square didn't frighten us. Newcastle's players were delighted to have got a goalless draw in the first leg at Sunderland especially, when Paul Hardyman missed a last minute penalty.

I was brought down for the spot-kick – it was definitely a penalty. I was in a position to score coming in on the angle of the box when Mark Stimson brought me down. I was a bit frustrated not to score myself and give us a goal lead to take to Newcastle, but as it turned out I got one at their place.

Paul Hardyman's penalty record was pretty good, but it was just a terrible penalty and he made matters worse by trying to kick John Burridge [The Magpies' goalkeeper] and the ball over the line. He was sent off for that. It came in the last seconds of the game. Newcastle were hyped up by that. They were full of it and I'm sure they thought they'd done the job. Our dressing room was quiet. You went in and it felt like a missed opportunity, even though the game had been pretty tight with not too many chances for either side. At first we were disappointed, but then we saw the funny side of what Paul had done and before we split up that day we said that it was our away form that got us to where we were and we would go there and take them on.

Even if it had been 1-0, I don't think we'd have gone there looking to keep it tight for ninety minutes. We weren't world class players at the end of the day and to defend for ninety minutes in a game of that magnitude you had to be pretty good. We were an attacking side. That 1-1 result against them on their own turf earlier in the season gave us good reason to fancy ourselves. In fact because we were such an attacking side we thought we had a really good chance. We knew they'd have to come at us a little bit, which would leave gaps and I knew I had the beating of Kevin Scott. He used to get very frustrated when he played against me and gave away a lot of free-kicks. I had too much movement for him, and along with Eric Gates' vision, we knew we could cause them problems.

We could attack like no other team in the division; going forward we were very good. It wasn't that we had poor defenders, it was just that our mentality as a team to go forward and attack, so we used to leave ourselves a bit short and susceptible to the break.

We couldn't have had anything better than an early goal at St. James' Park. It was a simple goal really. I fed Gary Owers, who got the ball into the danger area and Eric got on the end of it, he stuck his leg out and it went in.

We had good players. Gary Owers, for instance, had great energy and Gordon Armstrong would do well for us on the flank. The ball very rarely went out of play when we went wide. We played a lot of diagonal balls that Gordon could just head back across. They were good balls for me because the angle changed when the long diagonal was headed inside. That ploy always had defenders moving and turning and we enjoyed playing that way.

When we got the ball, we didn't just get rid of it. We played very cannily that night. We didn't just defend, but produced some good football. When we won it back, although pace-wise I was an outlet and it could be hit over the top for me, we had players who could just keep the ball, players who were comfortable in possession and who could keep it and relieve pressure.

We always knew there was another goal in it for us and when it came right near the end it was the perfect 'G Force' goal. I think it was Warren Hawke who had it wide. I always used to like to come off and get faced up to the centre-half. I came off and made it possible to turn. I didn't like to play with my back to goal. They had plenty of men back, so I came off and got short. When you're the type of player that runs with the ball, you put your head down and people think you're greedy, but the fact of the matter is when you're running fast with the ball and going past people you're looking at where the next tackle's coming from.

Eric was a master, whenever I got that split-second to look up, he would always be available. I went past one and he came off his markers a yard, so I played it for him. He'd always put it in a space for me to run onto. He did so this time, but I was wider than I thought and on my weaker side, although I always thought I was pretty decent with my left foot... I caught it nice, didn't blast it. I knew Burridge couldn't get near it. I was only about nine or ten yards from touchline, but the angle was a good 15 yards across goal. It seemed to take an age to go in. I remember wheeling away, thinking, "Is it going in or what?" There was just that split second as I was turning away to celebrate when I thought it might hit the post. It was a perfect goal, though, and there is a good photo of it.

It was a great moment. I wheeled away towards the main stand and our bench. All these people started to step out of the paddock towards me, so I thought, "No. That's a bad idea," so I ran more to the middle of the pitch! A load of the Newcastle crowd came onto the pitch and we were stuck in the middle of all the commotion. It was not very nice. Gary Bennett got off as quickly as he could! He was chucking people in red and white shirts behind him as he sprinted off!

We went up the tunnel as we sprinted off to safety, Newcastle's players went into their dressing room with their heads down. It wasn't like Roker Park! We were still celebrating the goal. We were still excited and didn't actually go into our dressing room. We just stood in the tunnel area. When you are at the dressing room end of a tunnel you can't really see that much, just what is right in front of the tunnel and all we could see was people running backwards and forwards. We daren't stick our heads out – we'd have got them knocked off! We were off the pitch for quite a while. We were asking George [Referee George Courtney] how long was to go. He said, "There are four minutes to go and don't worry we'll be going out to finish it." We were starting to think, "If we can't finish the game, what will happen then?" so that was a relief.

I can't remember much about what happened when we eventually got back onto the pitch, but I recall Eric played left wing for the last few minutes because he wanted to get off the second the final whistle went! It was just a case of seeing it through. We had a two goal cushion and they'd have had to score twice in a very short space of time and that just wasn't going to happen.

Pitch invasions do upset players. I experienced it again a few years later at Millwall when I was at Derby. Once again it was in a Play-off semi-final. It isn't a nice feeling when you're on the field and the crowd come on. You don't usually feel threatened, but no matter how much you can handle yourself, if ten to twenty people grab you, you don't know what's going to happen. It can be nerve-wracking. The invasion at St. James's took the sparkle off the night a little bit, but we achieved the result we wanted.

I get embarrassed about that night really because it wasn't as if it was a Cup final, and we didn't win anything. Sometimes I think it's overplayed. As a young lad I didn't really support a club, although sometimes I'd go and watch York. I played so much footy that I never had the time. So I didn't appreciate what it meant to supporters. I knew the north east derby is a special thing bragging rights wise. But since then I've realized a bit more about just how much, as that goal was a long time ago, but supporters always seem to come back to that game.

It's weird because we have people coming over to stay at our hotel, and they obviously haven't realized that it is me that runs it when they booked.

Sometimes they're standing there with their kid who's say about 12, and they're going, "This is Marco – he scored against the Mags," to their kid who wasn't even born, but even so, they know who I am and they know about the goal.

Sunderland supporters were always brilliant to me. If I hadn't scored, they wouldn't have thought differently of me because they had taken to me anyway, but that goal has become folklore. I think I scored better ones, but I know if I go back to Sunderland in thirty years time that's the goal they'll still be talking about!

Beating Newcastle put us into the Play-off final against Swindon at Wembley where we had a complete disaster from start to finish. With hindsight we made a massive mistake by going away on an end of season trip. If we did it now we'd get shot. We had a ten to twelve day gap between the semi-final and the final which was on a Bank Holiday Monday. The game really was a disaster. We were set up wrong. They played the ball out from the back and Denis [Sunderland manager Denis Smith] had Eric and me trying to chase it. That certainly wasn't Eric's game and the pair of us were shattered. They passed through us. The rest of our team were back on the half-way line and if they did win the ball back we were knackered.

Swindon outplayed us on the day and it's a good job Tony Norman had a blinder in goal for us. We were battered. I don't think we even created a chance. It was one of the most humiliating days I ever had in football. We just weren't at the races at all. Denis was a good manager and we usually did things in a good way, but on that day we were totally set up wrong and we didn't do anything about it during the game either. We just kept on trying to do the same things. We kept trying to win the ball off them up front, while they were playing 4 v 2 against me and Eric Gates and making us look like dummies.

That was probably why I got injured, it was frustrating. The ball got played into an area where the goalkeeper was always going to get it and I stuck my foot in out of frustration and ended up hurting my ankle. It was a really bad day. I'd done as well as I could, but I picked up an injury to the point where I was struggling for pre-season for the next year. I should have come off. If we had missed a few chances at least we might have felt we had given them a game. It was a total nightmare – to the point where I've blanked most of it from my memory.

I've played in other Play-off finals and got beat, but at least I've come off thinking at least we did ourselves justice in terms of a performance, but things conspired against us. I went to watch Sunderland play in the 1998 Play-off final against Charlton, the amazing 4-4 one where Sunderland lost on penalties and, although the lads lost, you came away thinking that was one of the greatest games I'll ever see. Both teams did all they could.

I was really gutted after the Swindon game. I thought we had a good team who usually played good football and personally I thought I was ready for the top league. We had no idea that we might end up being promoted as a result of Swindon's off the field problems. When that news came through, I was on a cruise ship in the Caribbean. My wife Debbie had won a competition a few years earlier, a Miss Yorkshire Evening Press thing. She'd won a cruise and never got round to doing it. So we'd finally got round to it as a way of forgetting all the disappointment.

Rumours started about the possibility of us being promoted before I went on holiday. There was talk of various scenarios. Of course being on a cruise ship I couldn't even get a paper, but I'd got talking to the crew on the boat because I needed to know. In the end I got a message from a ticker tape thing on the ship and I stood there watching it click past waiting for the news to come through! It was some way to discover you'd been promoted to the top flight.

With it being the strangest of promotions it was already the middle of June, which meant we only had a few weeks to prepare. Suddenly the fixtures were out and they gave us a first home game against Spurs, with Lineker and Gascoigne straight after Italia 90. I was very excited.

Before that, though, we kicked off the season away to Norwich where I scored my most memorable goal for Sunderland. It was my first top flight goal as well. Although I'd been doing well before then, you're never quite sure whether you're going to be able to do it at the top level. To crack that on the first day was terrific for me, but the way that game went turned out to sum up our season.

We were one of the most watched teams. So many home teams had their biggest crowd of the season against us partly because we had a big away support and partly because they knew they'd see a really good game of football – and that they'd probably win. We played open attacking football, but usually we would fall just too short. In five of our first six games we managed to score twice, but we only won one of those matches for instance.

I thought it was a shame how it all happened. We didn't have a very big squad which was the downside of last minute nature of our promotion. We brought in Kevin Ball and Peter Davenport to replace John MacPhail and

Gatesy, so we hadn't really increased the squad at all and then we had a few injuries. Kaysie was out for a while and we struggled for a right-back. A young lad called Paul Williams had to cover. He got tortured at Man United by Lee Sharpe, which was a shame because he was a good player, but we hadn't enough back up. We didn't do enough to keep us in the league as far as new signings went. I remember the transfer deadline approaching and thinking, "we'll sign someone soon," but it just didn't happen other than the arrival of Brian Mooney, who didn't play many games.

I remember being frustrated as a young ambitious player. I had a fairly decent season, I scored some good goals against Chelsea, Norwich and Everton. We had good players who were capable enough for it. There was the nucleus of a good young side with players such as Gary Owers, Gordon Armstrong, myself, Benno, Brace, Bally and so on – all players who played for a long while at a decent level. It was a strange season with the trip to Man City at the end. I still can't believe we got beat in that game. It was absolutely amazing. Even though we were threatened with going down, our fans meant that the gate that day was even bigger than what City'd had had when they played Man United. It was the same as the opening day of the season in that we played well, looked a threat – and still lost 3-2!

Denis Smith got the sack half-way though the following season, but by then I'd left myself. Denis was the only manager I played for at Sunderland. He and Viv Busby were good to play for. I'd been with them for about eight years from starting at York as a young lad. It was good to have Viv as a coach because he'd been a striker and he understood what it was like to play up front. He could put his arm around your shoulder and say, "It is tough," but he could be hard when he needed to.

Viv and I probably were among the more fiery characters and from time to time would fall out in training. Sometimes I used to get a bit too wound up and take things seriously all the time. With hindsight I sometimes shouldn't have got so wound up in training. He always used to say I looked tired. My argument was that I was tired because I was doing so much running! We used to do extra fitness work, which was never a problem for me, but I then had the demeanour of looking tired because I was! But if the ball came to me I'd be off again!

Denis always made training fun and enjoyable, but we used to work hard. You always had a ball at your feet, but without realizing it you would cover a lot of ground. We used to do a cross and finish session where you used the full pitch with two goals and two goalkeepers. They would be really good sessions and because you had the ball at your feet you enjoyed it. He used to organise nights out and join in social get-togethers with the boys. We were all fairly straight with each other.

I was at Sunderland in the early part of my career. It might surprise you to know that I was actually at Derby for longer than I was on Wearside. I didn't quite score so many goals for them, but I played more games. I don't go back to Derby as much as I do to Sunderland, though. They don't have as many groups of fans in different areas having social dos like they do at Sunderland. As a player at Sunderland you could be out every night of the week at some function or other. It was an enjoyable part of being at the club because the fans were so much a part of things. I know I'm held in high regard at Derby as well, but out of all the clubs I played for Sunderland is the one where I first hit the headlines. I scored twenty odd goals three years on the trot and obviously I was more than pleased with that.

I scored three hat-tricks for Sunderland, but managed to get myself sent off in completing the first of them! We were playing Ipswich at Roker Park. I'd already scored twice, when I took a penalty at the Fulwell End. The keeper parried my shot, but I was first to the rebound and tucked it away. Just as I did so, I got well and truly clattered by their defender Tony Dawes. I didn't deliberately elbow him – he ran into the back of me. If someone does that your first reaction is to try and shrug them off, but as I turned round I caught him with my elbow. I couldn't believe it when I was sent off – it was bizarre. If I'd cracked him, or had committed a bad foul I could have understood it.

The next time I got a hat-trick I managed to stay on the pitch to celebrate! It was against Watford and it was a good treble. Eric had possession on the left wing, played it into Colin Pascoe, who stunned it back to me and I smacked it. It was one of those that stays six inches above the ground straight into the goal. It was a beauty! The second goal of those three was a strange one. From a long through ball the defender tried to let it run to his keeper without passing it back to him. The keeper was about on the penalty spot, while the defender stopped with the ball still about six yards outside the box. I went round him and chased it, it was almost a tackle as I lunged for it, but it went past the keeper. For my third I actually flicked the ball on for myself and then raced for it. The keeper came out and I put it around him.

My third hat-trick came the week before I was transferred and all three came in the space of six minutes. It was away to one of my lucky teams, Charlton. I must have scored ten goals against them in my career. The goals came just after half-time. We'd had loads of chances in the first half, but hadn't put them away.

I did get another hat-trick in Sunderland, but it was against Sunderland at The Stadium of Light. It was in Jimmy McNab's Testimonial and it provided me with a real flashback, even though I'd left the club long before they moved to the new stadium. I played football at some fantastic clubs, but they seemed to move into brilliant stadiums just after I left. Derby did it, Sunderland did it. Even Darlo did it; so to go to The Stadium of Light was exciting. I scored some good goals that night even if the goalkeeper was Niall Quinn! I heard he was a very good keeper, so don't take the mickey! He saved a penalty from Dean Saunders, when he was at Manchester City once. I don't think even Thomas Sorenson would have saved them. It was quite a good hat-trick and I loved every minute of being back at Sunderland.

I had some great times at Derby as well. We were so close so many times to great things, but we got promotion in the end. One of my most memorable games was when I was captain against Sunderland the day we went top of the league. I scored in that game. It was ironic in a way, but it was a great occasion. It was at the Baseball Ground and there were a lot of Sunderland supporters there. I was lucky to play for two such great clubs.

At Palace, who I briefly played for between my time at Sunderland and Derby, it was horrendous. I hardly dared speak to people in the dressing room or in the bar afterwards. There was too much snootiness there. It wasn't like at Sunderland where players got on. At Sunderland we had older players who lived different kinds of lives, but those older players were still part of things.

We had some great characters at Sunderland such as Tony Norman, John Kay and Bally. Bally could scare you if he got that throbbing vein in the side of his head and he could give you a serious bollocking with about twenty swear words, but a minute or two later he'd be clapping his hands at you and shouting, "well done, well done." Kaysie, of course, is well documented as someone who would always be at the centre of any laughs, while Tony Norman was a quiet lad, but when he had a point to make he could make it count and he was a calming influence as a goalkeeper.

For a young player in my position when I came to Sunderland Eric Gates was a good player to have around. He showed me the ropes. Eric and I were on the same wavelength and I think Eric knew our partnership was good for him as well. A lot of players see another striker as a threat because you are competition for each other. If you've got four strikers at a club, usually only two of them are going to play. He was coming to the end of his career, but he realized that our partnership was good for both of us. We didn't actually get paired together to start with. It was only when Keith Bertschin got injured that we were put together. Eric was a great footballer with a lot of skill. He was a character off the field and was always involved in everything.

When I got to the age Eric was when he was partnering me I got a second wind. You realize your career is nearly over and you want to make it go on that bit longer. I definitely felt like that. I felt I should be playing at a better club in my last few years.

I never quite got the chance to play alongside my brother Ricardo, which would have been a dream come true for both of us. His one first team appearance for Sunderland ironically came when he came on as a sub for me at Leeds. He'd followed me from York where we had both been youngsters. He got dumped on a bit when I left York. Bobby Saxton was manager there at the time and, when I left, I think he had the feeling I'd been tapped up by Denis Smith, which definitely wasn't the case. Ricardo scored something like fifty goals at youth and reserve team level at York in the year they got relegated, but just about every other young professional except Ricardo had an opportunity in the first team. Bobby is a well respected coach, but he should have given Ricardo a chance.

Ricardo came to Sunderland when he was about nineteen. He was a 'younger' 19 than I was, but he was a good footballer. It was a shame that he didn't get a bigger chance than he did, but it was a bigger shame that when he did well on loan to Blackpool, Denis promised him football when he came returned to Roker, but didn't really deliver for him and then released him at the end of that season. He'd scored something like six goals in a month on loan with Blackpool and they wanted to keep him, but Sunderland wanted money for him. He was a bit of an unlucky lad. He went to Hartlepool the year they got promotion, but then Cyril Knowles the manager died and David McCreery took over and released him. He went to Carlisle, did well and got a contract but then broke his jaw. McCreery then came in at Carlisle and released him again. He's a very happy young man now and he's doing well in the hotel trade.

These days I run the Bishops Hotel in York. I came out of football with four young children and I didn't want to be doing anything where I was going to be away from the family whether it be in business or football. As a player with the hours I worked I was able to see our kids at all of their sporting events and so on. I'd never miss anything to do with them and to me that is one of the biggest privileges of being a footballer. For the next few years, until they all get their independence, the hotel fits in perfectly with that.

Whether the hotel is my long-term future or not, I'm not exactly sure. I wouldn't rule out getting back into football eventually. I wouldn't presume I could just walk back into a job. It would be very difficult to get back in. I know there would be a lot of time to invest in doing various courses, but we'll see.

I had a long playing career. I was lucky injury-wise. I never missed a game with a muscle injury – it was just cartilage problems and a groin problem I had. It was what became known as 'Gilmour's groin' as made famous by Gazza. I went to see Dr. Gilmour and he said it was the classic injury, but basically I'd recovered from it by the time I went to see him so there was no need to operate.

In the end it became an obsession that I had to be out there every week. I only missed the first game of the season once in twenty years and that was the last season I played. I think that's an achievement. Managers came and went, but even if I wasn't their cup of tea, I always made sure I was the one to get picked in the first team at the start of the season. The highlight for me is amount of games I played and always being involved. You see a lot of players who played around 300 games in their career and I managed over 650 just in the league.

When I look back at it I always feel a little tinge of regret that we didn't finish the job in the 1990 Play-off final. Over my career I played in four or five Play-off finals and didn't qualify once. They weren't very good times for me and I always look back at them with a little bit of regret and anguish that I never seemed to fall lucky in them. Worse still, I lost Play-off Finals, but never made a Cup final. The FA Cup was a disaster for me I never ever seemed to get a run – to the extent that I joined Palace the year after they got to the Final and left Sunderland they year before they did it! I can't look back and worry about that, though. I had a great career and Sunderland was a very important part of that.

TONY NORMAN
GOALKEEPER 1988–1995

BORN   24 February 1958, Mancot, Flintshire
SIGNED   29 December 1988 from Hull City £220,000 plus player exchange with Iain Hesford and Billy Whitehurst joining Hull. Valued at £450,000, Tony became Sunderland's record signing
SUNDERLAND CAREER   227 games
HONOURS   5 full Wales caps, 1 Wales 'B' cap, 2 Wales U18 caps, Play-Off Finalist 1990, FA Cup Finalist 1992
LEFT   Free transfer to Huddersfield Town, 6 July 1995

A consistent goalkeeper who gave excellent service to Sunderland. Signed shortly after playing a blinder for Hull against Sunderland, Tony would give numerous such displays for Sunderland, not least at Wembley in the 1990 Play-off final where, after producing a string of fine saves, the only way Norman was conquered was from a wicked deflection. Always a very calm and assured keeper, Tony spread confidence through his defence.

Sunderland 0 v Swindon Town 1

Second Division Play-off final
Monday 28 May 1990

Wembley Stadium
Attendance 72,873

Beaten only by a deflection, Tony restricts dominant Swindon to a single goal win. But Sunderland find themselves promoted anyway, when Swindon are punished for financial misdemeanours

Teams

Denis Smith	**Managers**	Ossie Ardiles
Tony Norman	1	Fraser Digby
John Kay	2	David Kerslake
Reuben Agboola	3	Paul Bodin
Gary Bennett	4	Alan McLoughlin
John MacPhail	5	Colin Calderwood
Gary Owers	6	Jon Gittens
Paul Bracewell	7	Tom Jones
Gordon Armstrong	8	Duncan Shearer
Eric Gates	9	Steve White
(Sub. Thomas Hauser)		
Marco Gabbiadini	10	Ross MacLaren
Colin Pascoe	11	Steve Foley
(Sub. Brian Atkinson)		
	Scorers	McLoughlin 27

Referee: J Martin

THE 1990 PLAY-OFF FINAL against Swindon Town was my first time at Wembley. Due to the aura that surrounded any sporting occasion at the old Wembley stadium it made it a special day, but for me personally I looked past the trimmings and just treated it as a typical match which was our route into the top division. Obviously to play at Wembley was a massive bonus and any professional's dream, but all that mattered to me was getting the result we needed.

We'd got through the Newcastle play-off games, which were massive occasions. Drawing nil-nil at home and winning two-nil away at Newcastle was fantastic for all the Sunderland people. It gave everybody in the club and the supporters a big lift, but to me the job was only half done and it counted for nothing if we didn't beat Swindon in the showpiece final. All I could think about on the day was winning. It was just the way I looked at every game.

There were 72,000 people there. Wembley was choc-a-bloc with Sunderland fans, including thousands along the legendary Wembley Way as we approached on the coach. There was a great atmosphere going down to the game that built you up and increased your expectations for it. It was a game of football for which, I felt, as a team, we were ready. And looking at it I think both sides were evenly balanced. But on the day it just didn't turn out that way at all.

We had a cracking day for the Final, the weather was beautiful. We knew it was going to be hot and we were going to have to work extra hard and everyone says Wembley's a bigger pitch – although, being a keeper, I was unaware of the impact of that. To me an 18 yard box is 18 yards, and a six yard box is six yards!

The game kicked off. I thought, "off we go" and the nerves settled – because everyone was nervous, the crowd and players alike. For the first five minutes we were alright, but after five minutes Swindon got into their stride and started to play their passing game that they were renowned for under manager Ossie Ardiles. To be fair, on the day, Swindon played some excellent keep-football and used the ball to great effect. In the conditions and over the 90 minutes, we simply didn't have an answer for them.

We seemed to add our own problems in a way. We gave a couple of bad back-passes, which for some reason were played blindly and just weren't on, that put us under unnecessary pressure. That maybe affected a little bit of confidence as well and, from then on, we gave the ball away very cheaply. I watched the game two years later and I remember thinking, "why did he do that?" on a few occasions. But we did make those mistakes and it just added to Swindon's momentum. We were shooting ourselves in the foot and they began to make their own chances through good play. We went through 20 minutes of mayhem, but we weathered it and hoped we would come through it to start playing ourselves.

The problem was they were still keeping the ball – every time we got it we were playing long balls out from defence and it kept breaking down. Back they came through the midfield and playing the ball out wide, causing us huge problems. Credit to them, they were dominating the game – but they hadn't scored yet – and I remember thinking about half an hour into the game, "Is that all your chances now? Have you used them all up yet?"

And then it happened. McLoughlin – I can still see him – picking the ball up in midfield. I thought, "Go on, hit it!" He was 25 to 30 yards out just to the right. He did hit it and the ball started to travel – and I was waiting for it. I knew where it was going: right hand, nice height. I had it covered. But then Gary [Bennett] put his foot out, in sheer instinct, which, as a defender, it was a natural thing for him to do. Instead of the ball traveling to my right hand side at a nice height, the way the ball clipped Gary's left leg it looped up and deviated to the left and was gone. My momentum took me further and further away from where the ball was now going. From then on it was slow motion – I can remember lying on the floor and watching it thinking, "This is going to be close," but I knew it was more in than out. It looped up and went in.

Looking back, I was always involved in the game. I referred to a spell of mayhem, which sums it up. Bad back-passes put us under pressure, but Swindon had a couple of chances where the luck went my way. One in particular where the ball was pulled back and I seem to remember Swindon's forward, Steve White, had a couple of good chances. There was one chance where the ball came across from the left and fell to White in the middle of the goal. But I'd come across to the centre of the goal from the right as he hit it. If he'd put it back into the corner where I'd come from, he'd have scored. But I was already moving to the left and saved the ball with my feet.

There are a couple of other saves that stick in my mind. For one, their lad shot from just inside the box, but I was perfectly positioned. There was another down to my right in the second half. They crossed it, headed it and I pushed it over the bar. It was a question of making the saves and hoping we could gain some impetus in going forward to take the game to Swindon. But that never happened.

The second half, due to us chasing the game, seemed to pass incredibly quickly and I remember jumping over the hoardings behind the goal in order to retrieve the ball after it had gone out of play for a goal-kick (Those were the days where there was only one match ball unlike today where numerous match balls are dotted around the play area). But despite all the effort, we just didn't get going, we didn't get into it. We had one or two half chances, but there were mistakes we made in the first half especially. There was a little bit of luck involved in us not going behind earlier, as to the rest of it – I had saves to make, but they were there to be made. If I hadn't made them I would have been disappointed.

I'd heard supporters say that they felt Swindon might not go up even if they won because of the financial controversies surrounding them at the time, but I never thought that would happen for a moment and they didn't play as if they thought that. I can't speak for everyone, but for me it never entered my head. Why think like that? You're seriosly playing and thinking, "don't worry, if we get beat there's still a chance"? For me the match was our chance.

We'd beaten Newcastle in the semi-finals of the Play-offs, but I don't look at the whole thing as two ties, I look at it as one. Newcastle being the first half and Swindon being the second half. And we lost. People come up to me and say, "Oh wasn't it great when you beat Newcastle?" and I say, "It was for nothing." What did we get? Nothing. That's how I look at the whole play-off situation – as a one-off. I found losing hard to bear.

It was after the Swindon game that speculation started to mount about whether they would be promoted or not. Immediately after the match the press wanted to talk about the game, but of course a week later, the season finished. And suddenly the Swindon situation is the topic of all the talk. In the back of my mind I obviously gave it more than a passing thought in the hope that, maybe for want of a better saying, we could get promoted 'through the back door'. But then I thought, "No you have lost your chance". The impact of winning the Newcastle game was gone. But we waited... a few days before it was announced I started to listen to the radio and I remember where I was when I heard the news. I was in the back garden with the radio on. It was a beautiful summer's day in Durham and it was announced that Sunderland had been promoted! I got a phone call from the club saying come down to Sunderland we're all attending the opening of a new club shop. Players and staff were there and we shared a glass of bubbly or something. It was just weird – from being totally dejected to discussing promotion!

From a player's point of view we were promoted through the Football League's rules, so technically we were promoted on merit. I'd swap it to have got promoted properly and to walk up the steps and get the trophy and walk all the way down, of course I would. In terms of getting promoted that would have been 100% – and the way we actually went up satisfaction-wise was about 50%. I would have loved to have gone up the other way – the normal way – but, after all, we went up. It was odd from then on. Instead of planning for another season in what is now the Championship we were preparing to go into the top flight.

The controversy over Sunderland being promoted rumbled on. Sheffield Wednesday had finished third bottom in the top flight and made a case for staying up. Newcastle had finished third in the Second Division and we'd finished sixth, but beaten them in the play-offs, and they argued they should take Swindon's promotion place.

Rules demoted Swindon. We played them in the Final – they won, but they couldn't get promoted, so there was only us left. I've got no qualms. If somebody comes up to me and says, "You should never have been promoted," I say, "I didn't make the rules." It would have been better if we'd won the game, but the way it happened, I have no qualms.

If somebody says Newcastle should have been promoted because they finished third my answer to that would be, "Don't tell me, tell the League to scrap the play-offs." It was nothing to do with Sunderland. If people are not happy with the system, why don't all the clubs say, "We're not happy. We're not going to have play offs. We want three to go up, and three to go down"? Newcastle bang on about, "Ah, but we finished third." Yeah, they did, but they didn't get promoted – if they wanted an automatic promotion spot, they should have come second. I am completely fine with it. I couldn't give a monkeys, because I know that the rules stated we should have been promoted. If Newcastle had been promoted instead I would have had a little niggle in the back of my mind saying, "they're not the rules." People say had we been beaten 4 or 5-0 by Swindon it might have been more difficult for the League to promote us, but we shall never know.

After all, we'd got to the Play-off final by beating Newcastle over two legs. They had played us four times that season and we never lost. We had the better of the two league games that were both drawn and the first leg of the Play-off semi-final at Roker Park. Hardy [Paul Hardyman] missed a penalty in the last minute and was sent off for following up. It finished 0-0 when we could have gone to St. James's Park 1-0 up. I personally feel that if we'd done that, the game at Newcastle would have been harder.

From a purely psychological point of view it would have been a harder game. As we walked to the dressing room after the first leg the Newcastle team were walking down one end of tunnel and we were walking down the other – and they're screaming, "Yes!" and sound ecstatic with the result. This for me was music to my ears. I loved it. In contrast we went in to our dressing room which was quiet and you could hear a pin drop with a feeling of dejection. I sat in my usual place by the door and I thought, "this is it." To me it felt like that door had just been opened as if to say, "Come on lads, fill your boots," that's how I felt.

Denis Smith never really had a proper go at anyone, but you could sense in the dressing room a feeling that we'd just let it slip. Denis said something about going to St. James' and I said, "I'll tell you something, we'll beat them there," and I think it was Paul Hardyman who piped up and said, "yeah, I think we'll beat them as well." I said it in such a way I think I took Denis aback. I could see him thinking, "He believes this," and I did. From the minute I heard them cheer I thought, "this is perfect, St James' Park here we go," because they thought they'd already done the hard part.

Going into the cauldron of the second leg, the atmosphere was red hot. I was thinking, "Come on – bring it on," because I just knew that their best shot on the day wouldn't be good enough. I knew psychologically we'd win.

We got an early goal through Eric Gates, held them comfortably and got the clincher through Marco [Gabbiadini] near the end. I can remember the crowd running onto the pitch. At first there were only one or two and then next thing there was a mad rush. I don't think half of them knew what they were doing. I understand their frustration at knowing their team was going to lose, but they didn't really know what they were running on the pitch for. I just walked toward the tunnel to get off and all these fans are running past me. And looking back I think, "how the hell I never got clattered…"

We were off the pitch for about twenty minutes or so and then came back out and played out the last four minutes. I saw those last minutes like another game. I didn't care if there were four minutes on the clock or another twenty. I looked at it as a third match, which I needed to keep a clean sheet in. That's the way I concentrated.

Looking at the Newcastle players. you could see that their heart had gone. We were doing our job. Our attitude was, "you're not going to score. If we're here and have to play you from now until midnight – we don't care how long it goes on – if the ball has to belted into row Z, it's row Z, we don't care. Now it's a four minute game and we're starting 2-0 ahead – you're not going to get that back in four minutes. It's a new game, the last game has finished." Newcastle's players were probably thinking exactly the same thing. It was impossible because the momentum of the main game had gone. They were thinking, "We can't do it," and were thinking, "We're not going to let you do it."

Newcastle never looked like scoring in that four minutes, but I never thought they were going to score at all during the entire 90 minutes. Even when Mark McGhee had hit the post earlier. I know this sounds funny, but when he hit it I thought, "That's not in." Sometimes when you're playing and you're on top of everything, the ball travels in slow motion and you have so much time to react. When you're having a bad game everything is so quick. After the game finished – yes we all enjoyed the result, the atmosphere, all the lads were on the bus, but from then I switched off again. It was gone, it was the Final that mattered now.

I was at Sunderland for almost seven years and the Play-offs were just a small part of that. There were a few other big games that stand out especially from the Cup run that took us back to Wembley for the 1992 FA Cup Final.

You're never aware that you are in a Cup run in the making. We'd beaten Port Vale and Oxford and had a Fifth round tie at home to West Ham. It was a scrappy game on a bobbly, hard pitch. We drew and went down to their place, which then was a tightly packed ground. We had a mixture of players at that particular time both young and more experienced and who were all basically good players. Not Pelés, but we had a good, solid team. Because of the way we were, the mix in the dressing room was superb. I think spirit is worth 20% before you even kick a ball. The humour that was within the squad took the edge off pre-match nerves. The camaraderie, everything; it just had that feeling about it. I can vividly remember before that game looking round the small dressing room with a physio's table in the middle as we were getting ready. It didn't matter if you were 17 or 35, everyone was treated exactly the same and could be on the receiving end of torturous leg pulling and banter!

It was a good game because both teams had a go. I remember David Rush giving 100%. You knew in that team, you'd get 100% from everybody. That's how it worked. It was 2-2 and then Rushie got the third. I just knew we were going to win. They had a young lad up front who had a couple of shots, but I was just in the right place at the right time. I look back and think, "Why were you there in the first place?" but it was just judgment. The [Tim] Breacker save everyone seems to remember. I remember him picking it up and having a crack. The ball just fizzes sometimes. He hit it, but instead of having any sort of spin on it, it kind of floated – the same panels on the ball faced me the whole time. I can remember going for it and it just kept going, it didn't dip at all. I thought, "this is close." As I've dived I thought I had to use my right hand to get to it. I was going for it with my left hand originally, but when I realized I wasn't going to get there with it, I brought my right hand over which allowed me that extra stretch and that's how it looked as if I'd suddenly managed to travel a bit further.

We stayed in London that night, sat in the hotel bar, and everyone was quiet due to physical exhaustion and pondering over the game we had just played and I think it was from then on we began to realize that we could be in the throes of a really good Cup run. The true realization dawned when we were drawn against Chelsea in the quarter-final. After gaining a good draw down at Stamford Bridge, we brought them back to Roker Park for the replay and the atmosphere that night made it a perfect footballing night. There was no wind, just a sort of mist that hung in the air. It was the perfect occasion for a good football match.

It was a pretty tight game. We scored and were in the driving seat. Chelsea had their chances. I can remember Kerry Dixon turning and hitting one across me and Dennis Wise headed it point blank, but I stood up and it came straight at me. Again right place, right time. That was an important save and for a long time it looked like we might just hang on and win 1-0. Then they got a late equalizer. But then we went straight up to the other end and Gordon [Armstrong] headed that fantastic last minute winner (I couldn't believe they didn't have a man on the back post defending the corner).

If somebody said to me now, "you played over 700 games over 21 years, what was the best atmosphere?" I'd say that Chelsea game. Without a doubt. It just had something on the night, better than Wembley even. This was the night where the players, staff and the supporters all thought, "This is it. It's officially a Cup run."

Looking back now, people remember the Chelsea game even more than they remember the semi-final against Norwich, even though we won the semi-final to get to Wembley. As for the Final itself against Liverpool, in the first half we were doing well, and had a couple of chances. Then after half-time they came out and scored fairly quickly and in the end they were deservedly comfortable winners.

We had started brightly, but they kept the ball and they were patient. Then they got the goal right at the start of the second half when Michael Thomas lashed one in from distance that arrowed perfectly into the top corner. For me playing in the game, when they scored you just knew they weren't going to give you one little look in, because their class was showing. I'm not afraid to say it, they were the better team by a mile and then Rushie [Ian Rush] just slotted one in.

Rushie had the knack, and I only know that because I actually trained with him with the Welsh national team. If a training game went dead, or if we were practicing free-kicks and a coach said, "hold it there" and the ball went anywhere near him, you'd just want to give him a clip around the ear because he'd just go for it and put it in the net. Just sheer habit – he had to do it, it was ingrained in him; a great teaching point for any aspiring forward. With Wales as well, of course, there was also another great striker in Mark Hughes. He must have been beaten up by a football when he was about three, because from then on he had to kick that ball so hard – he'd just leather it. Every time in training you'd see Hughsie about to take a shot at you, no matter if he was just a few yards away, you'd think, "Oh no, do I have to?" You knew you just had to spread yourself and I painfully remember saving the ball with my unfortunates on more than one occasion!

There were great characters in every team I played in, of course, and that was certainly the case at Sunderland. Everybody has their own character. One complemented the other. There was a mix of people and that was the beauty. You could have somebody who was very quiet and just listens a lot of the time, but when they speak everybody listens. Or you could have somebody go on and on all the time and you just switch off. Everybody was different character-wise.

At Sunderland John Kay, for instance, was a fairly quiet lad until he'd had a drink and then he wasn't! When you met him for the first time he was a lovely lad, but if you tried to run rings around him on a football pitch, he'd kick you. We used to call him 'Tut' because on the pitch he'd tut. Anything goes wrong and he tuts. He was great; I had a lot of respect for him. We really got on; he was great to have in the dressing room. He was as daft as a brush. He wasn't bothered. If you were out on a lads night out, he'd do something daft. We stayed over after a game once and one morning everyone got up and Denis [Manager Denis Smith] was there. He sort of looked and must have known straight off who'd been out and had a bit too much. He said, "Just had the hotel on to me saying something about plants." Straight away Kaysie jumped in, "It wasn't me!" No-one had even said anything to him! He had a habit of asking everyone: "I was alright, wasn't I?" From then on it was a standing joke this story about the plants. When he broke his leg against Birmingham in 1993, which effectively ended his professional career, we were all just gutted for him.

After so many years the majority of that Cup team met up for the Masters six-a-side tournament. It was fantastic to meet up with everybody and families alike. We all congregated outside the dressing rooms with families acting normal and catching up with news. Then when we went into the dressing room and that door shut, straight away it was like turning the clock back and the banter and stick started. "Are you still wearing that?" and "You've put on weight, we'll have to call you fatty." Everybody started giving everybody stick. It was great.

Our first game comes along and out we go. Within 30 seconds Kaysie gets in a tussle and he lands somebody on the floor after having a quiet dig in their ribs. The referee spots him and comes over and he tuts. Priceless!

Like I said, everybody had a character to add to the team spirit. For example Paul Hardyman was a quiet lad, but he had his sense of humour and joined in. Peter Davenport – Trainspotter – didn't drink. He was teetotal and he got stick because of it. He was called Ceefax because he could tell you anything. Then you had the three amigos: Don Goodman, John Byrne and Anton Rogan. When they came to stay at the Royal County in Durham it was like the OK Corral. When the three of them were together there was never a dull moment.

That there was such a great group of lads who could gel, get on together and play together was a great credit to the managerial staff of that time including Denis Smith, Viv Busby, Malcolm Crosby and Roger Jones. Like the players of this time, they all had different characters and attributes, which all contributed to the successes of the team at this time.

A year after the Cup Final we signed Alec Chamberlain, who I always got on great with. To be honest I've been lucky like that because wherever I've played I've always got on with the other goalkeeper. I got on well with John Davis at Hull, and then I moved to Sunderland and met up with Tim Carter. He must have seen me and felt a bit aggrieved because he'd done well and then in I came and took his place. But we got on well, worked together and encouraged each other. We were both stubborn and wanted to play in the first team, but whoever didn't play wished the other good luck. Nobody likes to be left out; if you aren't bothered you shouldn't be in the game.

I finished my football career at 39 years of age with Huddersfield in July 1997 when my contract ran out and I joined the Durham Constabulary as a Police Constable. I was there seven years in a variety of roles. Initially I did shift work in a patrol vehicle that included Friday and Saturday night duties with the Incident Reponse Team, which dealt with public order. I finally ended up, prior to my retirement, as a Beat Bobby. That suited me down to ground, getting involved with the community. During this time I always treated people the way I wanted to be treated. If it came to confrontation and it took five minutes to have a scrap, I'd rather spend 15 minutes trying to talk them down. Obviously there were occasions when reasoning didn't work. If they've had 28 pints then reasoning just doesn't work.

During the time I was serving as a police office I was also extremely fortunate to continue my contacts within football by coaching under 16 goalkeepers at the Middlesbrough Football Club Academy.

I was eventually medically retired from the Police Force in December 2004, after a long period of absence due to ill health. I first became aware that something was wrong with my health whilst I was on the beat and during the afternoons became increasingly tired and began to develop breathlessness when walking up steep inclines. After spending a period of eleven days in hospital after these symptoms had worsened and had three litres of fluid drained from the right-hand side of my chest that caused the right lung to collapse, I was diagnosed with having cardiomyopathy, which, in simple terms, damage to the heart muscle. When I was in hospital, the first two people to walk in were Steve Pears from Middlesbrough and Kevin Ball. The fella in the bed across from me was a Newcastle supporter, and his face dropped. I could see he was thinking, "I know him," and I could see he was desperate to ask. When I explained what I had been told to Kevin he got on to the PFA to see if they would finance a second opinion and they agreed to do so if needed.

After my release from hospital I then began a lengthy term of absence from work. It took a while for the diagnosis I was given in hospital to sink in, but slowly and surely it did and it came as a terrible blow. I have always tried in life to look on the bright side and towards the future, but to be sat in a hospital whilst a heart consultant explains to you that you have two choices, the first being a course of medication which could help you with a quality of life or if that fails to be considered for a heart transplant I found it difficult to cope with. I also had to finish my coaching at Middlesbrough.

In the meantime, during my absence from work I had a handful of welfare visits from police personnel and numerous visits to my doctors for sick notes and when asked by the doctor how long for I invariably said, "two to three weeks" in the vain hope that I could return to work.

After six months my monthly income was halved and I began to feel extremely isolated, which was exacerbated after twelve months when my income dropped to zero. I had to produce regular sick notes from my doctors and you could guarantee that if I didn't hand one in, there would be a knock on my door within 48 hours and it would be an Inspector or a Sergeant from the local police office asking for my sick note. Unscheduled absenteeism, you see. In my mind it was bad enough not being able to go back to work, never mind having someone chasing me for sick notes. I eventually gave up and asked to be issued with a sick note for 12 months. Nobody from the police actually ever asked what my condition was.

My welfare visits had seemed to come to an end, so out of sheer frustration I asked to be visited by my line manager who was an Inspector, whom I had never met. When he arrived he asked me the run of the mill question of what they could do to help me and, as they couldn't put me back on full pay, find me a job or give me a new heart I, in turn, I asked if he had any idea what my condition was and how long my sick note was for. He answered "No" to both questions and intimated that the only way forward for me was to seek medical retirement from the Force. That I proceeded to do and this took eleven months to come through.

Me being me and not being able to accept my condition and roll over I decided to set myself a goal by undertaking a challenge to walk 190 miles of Wainwright's West to East Coast to Coast walk from St. Bees in Cumbria to Robin Hood's Bay. It was a personal challenge for me. The walk took me 17 days, which I did alone (yes I know I've got no mates!) and raised a few bob for the Children's Heart Federation. I contacted Gordon Taylor at the Professional Footballers Association to let him know of my intention to do the walk and he wrote back and said the PFA would finance my accommodation as their contribution to the worthy cause. Unbelievable. I'd stopped playing, and therefore being a member, ten years before and they've not only offered to pay for a second medical opinion, they sponsored me on the walk as well. The PFA said, "You're a past player, and regardless of what you've done in the game and how long ago you retired, you're a past player and you're a member of the PFA."

People often ask me how being in the police compares with football. They are absolutely light years away from each other is the answer. In football – you've got your Chairman, the Board, the Manager, Coaching staff, players and the staff that help run the place. That is compact and everybody relies on each other. In the police, you've got your local station, you've got Headquarters, the sub divisions and they've all got their little way of doing things and set patterns. Then you've got the Northumbria and Cleveland Forces and they're different.

In football, to get best out of players, the manager encourages them to work as a team and includes himself within that team, whereas, personally, I found in the police, once individuals get promoted and begin to move up the ranks it was a case of, "I'm alright Jack" and they lose touch with the team spirit they once worked with. I do believe in all honesty that certain people, as they rise through the ranks and lose their team spirit, tend to look after themselves to the detriment of others if need be. I just find the difference unbelievable.

I had a couple of cracking sergeants who were my direct managers. They took the time to know how you spent your working day and knew if you were a grafter. They would be the ones that would say to you after a long day, "get yourself away a little earlier" and in return it would be for them that you would readily change your shift from an 8 till 4 to a 6 till 2 in order to help out with any Operations that were ongoing.

After working in another environment following 21 years of playing professional football, I realised one of the beauties of football is that there is nowhere to hide, and when times are bad for someone it is up to their individual strength of character, and the support of his team-mates, to help him get through it. In the Police, probably like with any other profession, there could well be people who are quite happy to simply only do what they have to do and there are others who do more for more then just what is expected of them.

Out of everything that happened to me, I believe I was privileged to play the game and have a great career. When things didn't go as I'd have liked, I turned to the PFA and it made me proud to play the game. It does to this day. They have just been fantastic. It's the players that played 20-30 years ago that need help. When you're in the game you're watched over. If you give your best you're looked after. I look back knowing that I have been extremely lucky to play professional football for 21 years. I can highlight, as I have done, some of the memorable games that I have played in, but you never know how you are thought of by the supporters.

I can honestly say that my two most memorable moments in my career would be my first international cap for Wales and a second, that sums up the pride I have for my time with Sunderland Football Club. This would be when I returned to Roker Park with Huddersfield Town to play against Sunderland. I recall travelling on the coach when one of my Huddersfield team mates asked me the simplest of questions, "what sort of reception will the crowd give you?" To which I replied, "I don't know." At the beginning of the game I had to change ends from the Roker End to the Fulwell End and as I jogged down the length of the pitch the ovation I received from all corners of the ground was emotional and it was the proudest moment I had in football.

Footnote:

After a Football League investigation, Swindon's chairman Brian Hillier admitted to 36 charges of breaching league rules, while their Financial Director and former manager Lou Macari were also accused of being involved in the fraudulent activities which had been going on at the club. While Hillier was eventually jailed for fraud with the Finance Director receiving a suspended sentence, the club's footballing punishment saw the League promote Sunderland to the First Division in Swindon's place. Initially the Robins even lost their place in the Second Division to Tranmere Rovers, who'd lost the Third Division play-off final 2-0 to Notts County. But Swindon appealled and were reinstated to Division Two, a decision which, understandably, infuriated Tranmere.

KEVIN BALL
CENTRE-BACK/MIDFIELD 1990–1999

BORN 12 November 1964, Hastings
SIGNED   11 July 1990 from Portsmouth; £350,000
SUNDERLAND CAREER   388 games 27 goals
HONOURS First Division Championship 1995/96 & 1998/99, FA Cup
Finalist 1992
LEFT Transferred to Fulham, 9 December 1999; £200,000
RETURNED to coaching staff 2003, Caretaker manager March-May 2006

Bally was Sunderland's Enforcer. He went on to become a Sunderland
legend with his commitment equalling anything any local player had ever
produced and making a mockery of the southern softie stereotype – no-one
surpasses his five red cards in a red and white shirt! After moving into midfield midway through his decade at Sunderland, he adapted brilliantly to the
position and captained Sunderland to the Football League Championship
in the promotion seasons of 1996 and 1999. Kevin returned to the club's
coaching staff in 2003 and was caretaker-manager from March to May 2006.

Sunderland 3 v Chelsea 0
_____

FA Premier League
Saturday 15 December 1996

Roker Park
Attendance 19,683

Sunderland outfight and outplay Chelsea in SAFC's first Premiership serason in the final campaign at Roker Park

Teams
_____

Peter Reid	**Managers**	Ruud Gullit
Lionel Perez		Frode Grodas
Gareth Hall		Steve Clarke
Dariusz Kubicki		Scott Minto
Paul Bracewell		Craig Burley
		(Sub. Roberto Di Matteo)
Kevin Ball		Michael Duberry
Andy Melville		Dennis Wise
Michael Gray		Andy Myers
(Sub. Steve Agnew)		(Sub. Mark Hughes)
Richard Ord		Frank Sinclair
Craig Russell		Ruud Gullit
Alex Rae		Gianfanco Zola
(Sub. Michael Bridges)		
David Kelly		Eddie Newton
Duberry (og) 30, Ball 47 Russell 67	**Scorers**	

Referee: M Bodenham

I ENJOYED SOME CRACKING matches as a Sunderland player. My debut against Spurs, for a start, was a thrilling game, although it was goalless. We'd just been promoted and more than matched a flamboyant Tottenham team with Gazza and Gary Lineker at their best straight after Italia 90. Then there was the 1998 Play-off final when we drew 4-4 with Charlton and then lost on penalties, despite scoring all of our first six! The walk to take my penalty at Wembley seemed like the longest I've ever done, but I had the relief of seeing it go in. We lost that game cruelly, but responded with a record 105 points to win the league the next year.

A couple of games against Chelsea also stand out for me. There was, of course, the incredible FA Cup quarter-final replay at Roker Park in 1992, when Gordon Armstrong scored a spectacular last minute header and we went on to reach the Final, but for me the 'Match of My Life' was actually a straightforward Premiership game against Chelsea.

We'd been relegated in my first year at Sunderland and had spent five years clawing our way back into the top flight, which by then had transformed itself from the First Division into the Premier League. Peter Reid had come into Sunderland as manager, saved us from relegation from what was then Division One and then won promotion in his first full season, with a team based on organization and defensive solidity, which was illustrated by the fact that our top scorer in a title winning year had just thirteen goals.

This game took place in our first season back in the top flight. We were doing alright for a promoted team at the time – we'd won four, drawn five, lost eight and were 15th in the league, but we'd been beaten 3-1 at home by Wimbledon the Saturday beforehand.

That season the BBC was doing a documentary series called *Premier Passions* which used to follow us about all the time. They'd have the cameraman in on the team talks before and after games and during half-time. Any time really. It was literally the proverbial fly on the wall documentary. I've seen documentaries in the past and seen what spin can be put on things, but seeing the outcome of Premier Passions, I thought it was superb. Funny thing was, on the Wimbledon day, the week before we played Chelsea, we didn't play particularly well. We were getting beat at half-time and we were expecting a roasting from Peter Reid and Bobby Saxton. As we went into the dressing room the cameraman and his flunky followed us in and I and remember saying to him, "I wouldn't f*****g come into the changing room if I were you", because I knew we were about to get a Reidy hairdryer. As he came in, Reidy said "and you f*****s can get the f*****g hell out of here!" So he'd given him even more expletives than I had, so the cameraman turned tail. The gaffer went on doing his half-time team talk, telling us 'politely' where we were going wrong and what we should be doing. You can understand that, with Reidy being the passionate person that he was, it was in no uncertain terms, and Sacko [assistant manager Bobby Saxton] had a go as well. When we walked out ready for the second half the cameraman had been outside and, having felt the walls rattling, he couldn't thank us enough for trying to stop him going in!

Wimbledon was a side that we'd have wanted to beat, even though they might have been doing well at the time. They were the sort of team we were looking to get something out of. So it was a disappointment to lose at home to them.. We then came up against Chelsea – a team full of big hitters, Ruud Gullit being one of them and Gianfranco Zola another – a massive team.

It was a lively start to the game. It was just before Christmas and there was a great atmosphere. I would imagine Chelsea came with the intention of giving Sunderland a good going over, but we had a bit of a role-reversal on the day. It was one of those games where you start the warm-up and you think, "yeah, I feel good today." You feel like you could run all day.

My goal came right at the start of the second half. We were one up at the break thanks to a Craig Russell shot that had taken a deflection off Michael Duberry on the half hour. At half-time they'd have re-grouped and felt they could get back into it, but going 2-0 up within a couple of minutes of the re-start had us flying and them bewildered. Russ deserved to get his name on the score-sheet and did so half-way through the second half, when he finished off a good move after Ned [David] Kelly and Brace [Paul Bracewell] had combined.

I just had a massive amount of energy in that particular match. I've watched the game on video since, and thought, "bloody hell, look at me, I'm absolutely non-stop – running all game." We were 1-0 up when, all of a sudden,I remember the play building up and Alex Rae knocked the ball out to Mickey Gray and on the video you can see me take off as the ball goes wide. Mickey Gray gets it wide-left and puts this lovely little cross in and there you see me at the far post to head it in.

But the funny thing was, as the ball came across, I was flying! I was absolutely horizontal – it's comical. I looked like Cooper-man, not Superman. I'm horizontal when I head it, but the momentum from when I headed it took me into the back of the net as well. Having ended up in the net after a diving header to put us 2-0 up against the Harlem Globetrotters of Chelsea, I thought, "hold up, this is what school-boy dreams are all made of!" To then stand up in the net and see all the Fulwell End screaming and shouting was brilliant. To see all the faces screaming and ranting and the passion that exuberated from them was fantastic. You feel it coming towards you – and it was a great feeling.

Prior to this game I'd missed what you would class as good opportunities in front of goal. When I spoke to our centre-half Andy Melville after the game, he told me, when I took off, he'd thought, "don't bloody miss this one." I had a little chuckle about that because what I'd done on the pitch had an impact on other people's performances and mental state. Years later I'd find that that goal left an indelible mark on the mind of one of the greatest players I've ever seen too.

The match culminated in us winning 3-0. Really Chelsea were never in it and if you look back at the stats from that game you'll see that for all their big name stars they never had a shot on target in the whole 90 minutes. They had bags of skill, of course. There was a little trick that Gullit did on me in the middle of the park, and I remember thinking, "I should've clattered him." It was a great bit of skill, but he wasn't going anywhere. There was another time I remember taking him on, and it's funny, because all of these things happened, but you had no fear. You had no fear of who we were up against.

The game was live on Sky TV and 3-0 was a handsome result. The family were all watching and then I was presented with the Barclays Man of the Match award. That was a fantastic feeling. Every time I go into the dining room at home – I don't go in there very often – there's a bottle of champagne in there that's never been touched. It's great because it just gives me a little reminder that I used to be able to run around at one time.

My goal itself was a great move, and it wasn't until five or six years later that the impact that goal had on someone came back to me. I was at Burnley at the time, playing a pre-season friendly. I'd been a naughty boy, so I was suspended for the first game of the season. Stan Ternent was our manager and, as a former coach at Stamford Bridge, he'd done great to get Chelsea up for a pre-season game. Because I knew I wasn't going to be playing the following week, I had really worked hard in training as well as on the day of the match – I did extra running and things like that. I was absolutely sharp, but I was on the bench. I thought, "he won't put me on today, I'll just enjoy the occasion." However, a shout went out just after half-time, "I need a centre-back, where's Bally?" and there I was behind the dugout thinking, "Christ, my legs are killing me, I'll never be able to run today." Stan said, "Bally, will you be able to go centre-back?" and I went, "yeah. No problem." So I went on the pitch.

The first players I came up against were Eidur Gudjohnsen and Jimmy Floyd Hasselbaink, who were playing up front for the Blues. So I'm thinking, "Christ. Here we go. I've got my work cut out for me here." Those two ran off ten minutes later and who should come on but Gianfranco Zola. And the amazing thing was, he came up to me and said, "Hello Kevin." I looked down – I was a little bit taller than him – and I said, "Alright Zola." And then he proceeded to say, "It's fantastic to still see you playing" and he was telling what a great professional I was. And then all of a sudden he went, "I remember the goal you scored against us at Roker Park." Now you're talking five or six years previously. He said what a great goal it was and I remember thinking he was taking the piss, but then he said, "I tried to catch you, but you were too fast," so I thought he was definitely taking the piss. But he then proceeded to talk me through the goal, and what a fantastic goal it was. Here he was. Zola. The guy was everything you'd want in a modern day professional footballer, and he was telling me what a fantastic goal I scored.

All this happened in a reasonably short period of time, and then he said to me that at the end of the game he'd like me to have his shirt. Now for someone of his stature to say that – the impact he had on me in that split second was enormous. I was so pleased that what I'd done as a player to him then, and subsequently, had had an effect on him. The fact that he admired a fellow professional impressed me and I remember saying, "I would love to have your shirt, it would be an honour. Thank you very much." And then I thought I'd return the favour and asked if he wanted mine, and he said he'd like that.

I still kicked the shit out of him in the second half – whenever I got near him.

What I tried to say to the players at Sunderland when I was caretaker-manager was that the impact you have on people's lives, you don't even realize at times. The impact I had on Zola's life was okay – we gave them a good hiding 3-0 at home and we thoroughly deserved to, but it would have a relevance later on in my career and it made me feel like a million dollars, I've never forgotten it.

Some time later I did a charity dinner with a young lady. I had nothing with me to donate to the raffle for a prize, but I had a pencil drawing that was done by one of my best mates, that was of me going past Zola of all people. So I wrote to Gianfranco at Chelsea and asked him to sign it, which he did. It raised four or five hundred quid. For a guy like Zola to take time out to get to know fellow professionals was tremendous. He went up so far in my estimation – he was already high anyway, but to go up again was phenomenal and I'll never forget that moment.

People don't believe I scored 27 goals for Sunderland, although they aren't slow to remind me I missed a fair few chances as well! Looking back, in terms of the game itself, who we were up against, the fact that we'd just been beaten at home by Wimbledon and that the Chelsea game was live on Sky, then my header against the Blues was a goal that midfielders dream about in terms of the ball goes wide, you break into the box and score with a diving header at the end where your home fans are congregated. You couldn't ask for anything better.

But some of the other goals I'd scored were pretty good goals. I think of a volley I scored in a Play-off game at Sheffield United, a goal away to Wolves when I volleyed into the top corner for a late winner and another volley at West Brom. That was the winner in a game where we came back from 2-0 down to win 3-2. One of the greatest goals I've scored was against Peter Shilton when he was at Derby County. The ball was headed out by Mark Wright, I took a touch and lobbed Shilton. When I look at some of my goals they provide a good contrast to some the of ones I missed, like an open goal at Spurs that still haunts me.

Of course, while I took my responsibilities to contribute goals from time to time very seriously, I was in the team mainly to stop them – whether I was playing centre-back and even after I moved into midfield, where my main role was to shield the back four. Like all midfielders I took a lot of satisfaction out of creating goals and, while someone like Gianfranco Zola would often lay goals on a plate for a team-mate with a sublime piece of skill, I made a few myself. One of the goals I took a lot of pleasure from was Kevin Phillips' goal in the 1998 Play-off final against Charlton at Wembley. I dived in for a header where the boots were flying and got a whack on the head, but that didn't matter when I saw Kevin Phillips latch onto my headed pass and go on to score.

That Play-off final lives in the memory because of all the emotions, and the subsequent aftermath and how that propelled the club forward. There are so many memories from my time at Sunderland, especially how I relished beating Fulham when I was caretaker-manager to finally win a home game in the terrible 2005/06 season, when we were relegated with only 15 points.

One other game that stands out for me is against Birmingham, in the last game at the Stadium of Light when we won the Championship in 1999. We were on 102 points and had sealed the title, but I was desperate to finish the season with another win. The day before that I had to go down to the FA because I'd picked up 15 bookings over the course of the season. My defence was that my job in the team was to kick people, to get the tackles in and be aggressive. I felt I was being singled out for the job I'd done. Other people didn't get booked for the same stuff that I did. If I caught someone it wasn't intentional, it was because I wanted to win the ball for our team. I told the disciplinary panel, "I'm the captain. I'm fronting this team and it's my job to do the tackling – they need me and I need them. They don't get penalized for what they do, but I might for what I do. If you look at it over the course of the year, I made at least 12-14 tackles per game, multiply it over 46 games. I've been booked 15 times, I think I've done pretty well really." And they looked as though to say, "What's this kid on about?" Then they sent me out and brought me back in and said, "Look we're not going to suspend you, but you'll be fined £3,000." So I had to pay three grand for the privilege of kicking people, but it allowed me to play in the game the next day. At half-time we were getting beat 1-0 and we weren't playing well, so I was fuming, because I was thinking about all the effort I'd put in yesterday at the FA and the fact that I'd wanted to get 105 points. We had a right moan at half-time, everyone was arguing, but it worked because we went out and won 2-1 to achieve the 105 points total. When I got back to the changing room I celebrated like I always used to: put my feet up and had a cup of tea. I was so relaxed afterwards because the job was done.

In all of my years as a player at Sunderland I came across some great characters, of course, and the team that beat Chelsea 3-0 was full of them. Lionel Perez was very flamboyant and very much the typical French keeper – very eccentric. Darius Kubicki and Scotty were the ultimate professionals – I still talk to Scotty now. Michael Gray came up through the ranks and Russ was another homegrown lad, Ordy had great feet, he could do things on the ball that I could never do. When I first came to the club I established a great rapport with Dickie Ord straight away. I remember running out in the hills round Maiden Castle when Denis Smith used to make us go on a pre-season run and me and Dickie came in last. Denis was always waiting for us, and he would say, "thank bloody god..." when we finally turned up and Dickie would be pissing himself.

Brace was again a model professional. Very straight-laced. He knew what he was on about. Alex Rae was a fantastic footballer, but had that Glaswegian edge about him. He loved to tackle hard. He wanted to win. He loved a laugh, but was a very good professional as well. Ned Kelly was brought in and didn't play for while as he was injured. The one thing we had above everything else was a tremendous team spirit. We got relegated on 40 points, which was a shame because if we'd just had a goalscorer who could get about eight or nine, we'd have stayed up. As it was, no-one scored more than four goals. We'd brought Niall Quinn in as well, but he was injured for nearly all of the season.

But there was always that team spirit. If a game was flat, Mary [Andy] Melville would shout, "Bally, go and do something. Go start something." In the end he would be actively encouraging me to tackle someone or whack someone or get involved in something that had absolutely bugger all to do with me. Just to get the lads and the fans going. I'd take the bait and rise to it, do something and raise the temperature a bit. He'd go, "brilliant" and the game would be up and running.

NIALL QUINN
CENTRE-FORWARD 1996-2002

BORN 6 October 1966, Dublin
SIGNED 15 August 1996 £1.3m from Manchester City (Club record fee)
SUNDERLAND CAREER 220 games, 69 goals
HONOURS Division One Championship 1998/99, 1 League Cup, 91 Republic of Ireland caps, 21 goals
LEFT Retired 10 November 2002
RETURNED as Chairman July 2006, Manager July and August 2006

As good a leader of the line as a centre-forward as the game has seen, Niall Quinn thrived in the north east, playing the best football of his life as one half of the country's most feared double-act alongside Kevin Phillips. After the record breaking promotion of 1999, the years that followed brought Sunderland's highest League finishes for half a century. Niall's popularity was immense and was added to when he donated £1m raised by his benefit match to hospitals in Sunderland, his native Dublin and also made a donation to charity for street children in India. In 2006 Quinn returned to Wearside, leading the Drumaville Consortium in buying the club and becoming Chairman. Key to the passion and character the Irishman grew to love at Sunderland was the response to the 1998 Play-off final, one of the most dramatic matches ever seen at Wembley.

Charlton Athletic 4 v Sunderland 4 (after extra time)

Charlton win 7-6 on penalties

Division One Play-off Final , Monday 25 May 1998

Wembley Stadium
Attendance 77,739 (Play-off final record)

Sunderland score 'ten' times and yet lose one of Wembley's greatest ever games

Teams

Alan Curbishley	**Managers**	Peter Reid
Sasa Ilic		Lionel Perez
Danny Mills		Darren Holloway
(Sub. John Robinson)		(Sub. Chris Makin)
Mark Bowen		Michael Gray
Neil Heaney		Lee Clark
(Sub. Steve Jones)		(Sub. Alex Rae)
Richard Rufus		Jody Craddock
Eddie Youds		Darren Williams
Shaun Newton		Nicky Summerbee
Mark Kinsella		Kevin Ball
Mark Bright		Kevin Phillips
(Sub. Steve Brown)		(Sub. Danny Dichio)
Clive Mendonca		Niall Quinn
Keith Jones		Allan Johnston
Mendonca 23, 71, 103 Rufus 85	**Scorers**	Quinn 50, 73, Phillips 58 Summerbee 99

Penalties: Mendonca 1-0, Summerbee 1-1, Brown 2-1, Johnston 2-2, Jones 3-2,Ball 3-3, Kinsella 4-3, Makin 4-4, Bowen 5-4, Rae 5-5, Robinson 6-5, Quinn 6-6, Newton 7-6, Gray (saved)

Referee: E Wolstenholme

WHEN I FIRST ARRIVED as the club's record signing a lot was expected of me and I think we got off to a good start. I had a goal disallowed on my first appearance as a substitute and then bagged a couple of goals on my first start in a big away win [4-1 at Nottingham Forest]. The season had only been going a few weeks, though, when I got a nasty cruciate injury in a game against Coventry. I'd had a cruciate injury before in my other leg, so I knew about the recovery period, but I worked my socks off. I came back far too early, because I was desperate to play against Newcastle. It was only something like four months and two weeks after the operation. We were 1-0 up for a long time, but it just didn't work out and the game ended as a draw, although David Kelly very nearly got the winner in the last minute. I was on one leg really. I played on until the end of the season, which ended with the drop after a 1-0 defeat at Wimbledon. I played, but I couldn't run.

People think I played through a lot of pain, but the problem really was one of maneuverability more than pain as such. You simply can't do what you'd normally be able to if you're fully fit. I was taking tablets and injections – all the things they tell you not to do. Peter Reid was the same, he came from that ilk, thinking that you could play even if you were only half fit. I can remember when I had a bad ankle before a game – it was well swollen – and Sacko [coach, Bobby Saxton]was saying to me, "you've got to play." I remember saying, "Bobby, I can't kick the ball," to which Sacko replied, "Since when do we ever want you to kick the ball? We just want you to head it. If we wanted someone to kick the ball, you wouldn't be in the team." So I played and we won that day. I was determined to make it back. I trained very hard. I didn't get back properly before the season ended, but it proved to be too little too late and we were down.

I had an operation in the summer of 1997 to clear the knee out, but it still wasn't right. I played a few games in the opening few weeks of the Stadium of Light and was fortunate enough to score the first ever goal there, but I was struggling and was on the verge of retiring, when I went for my last consultation. I had all my papers from the PFA, I was ready to quit football, but the surgeon, a Mr Bollen in Bradford, who the club still use, found the problem. It wasn't the original cruciate at all, it was something else in my knee. So he sorted it and I played again five or six weeks later, coming on against promotion favourites Nottingham Forest. It was the start for me at Sunderland where Peter Reid believed in me.

The next game that stands out for me was against Port Vale. That was the turning point. It doesn't sound great on paper, but there was a big crowd. I scored a particularly skilful goal – for me anyway. I chipped the goalkeeper, Paul Musselwhite, to make it 3-0 after about 20 minutes of a 4-2 win and that was it, it was a weight off my back. After that I scored my goals in batches. A hat-trick against Stockport, and pairs against both QPR and West Brom.

We'd given the other clubs a big lead. We were in the bottom half of the table at one stage, but we put a spectacular run together and gathered a ridiculous amount of points [90] to not gain an automatic promotion place. Bryan Robson's Middlesbrough and Frank Clark's Nottingham Forest just kept their noses in front.

I remember watching one game at the end of the season. Middlesbrough were just ahead of us and they were playing against a team who had a chance to score to equalise in the very last seconds of the match – it was a one-on-one with the keeper, and it went agonizingly wide. I fell off the couch watching it. Alan Brazil was doing the commentary and he said, "If there are any Sunderland players watching this, they'll have just fallen off the couch," and I thought "I have!"

We kept winning, but so did Boro and Forest. So the results cancelled each other out. It was a pity, but we had to go through the play-offs and ended up playing against Sheffield United in the semi-final. We played really well. Bally scored great goal to put us in the lead in the first leg at their place and we looked in control, but they nicked one back and eventually won the first game 2-1.

We were in good shape going into our home leg. There was a really smoky, foggy atmosphere at the Stadium of Light. I can remember things not going to plan, Sheffield United gave it a real good go and played really well, at one point forcing Lionel Perez to make an unbelievable double save. For all his faults, and in the Play-off final he was to make a big blunder, on that particular night he made a world-class save to keep us in it, and we got there in the end, managed to win the game 2-0 thanks to an own goal and one from my strike partner, Kevin Phillips, and we found ourselves in the Play-off final at Wembley.

That game, I can remember us probably playing the worst 45 minutes of football the club had played in a long, long time. At that stage, Charlton lead 1-0 thanks to a goal by their prolific striker Clive Mendonca, who had signed from Grimsby for a big fee the previous summer. You can put it down to nerves, people were freezing and we were unco-ordinated. Wembley and the occasion and all can do that to you.

The manager made a switch at half-time and brought Chris Makin on for Darren Holloway. Chris is a passer of the ball, a cultured full-back. We suddenly started getting the ball and passing it around and we found our way. We started to open Charlton up, and I have to say it was the most enjoyable 45 minutes I've ever played in. We absolutely controlled game, played some lovely football and had people on the edge of their seats. We were involved in a titanic struggle to finish three all at full-time. It regularly gets picked nowadays for the best game ever played at Wembley in these polls they have on Sky.

But we never should have been level. We were superb in that half and got ourselves in front with a couple of good goals. The first of my goals was a diving header to equalize at the near post from a corner. Kevin Phillips scored a great goal as well to make it 2-1 in our favour. For my second goal I chested the ball down and stuck it in. I was delighted with myself and was feeling good.

And yet we couldn't shake them off. Charlton broke a few times and got a goal to level it at 2-2 on the break totally against run of play. Clive Mendonca, of course, was a Sunderland lad. He was turning on a six-pence that day and he caused Jody [Craddock] and Darren [Williams] a lot of problems. Even though he didn't get much of the ball, when he did he was pretty hot. He was like Kevin, he only needed a sniff of a chance to latch onto the ball and bury it. He'd scored both their goals and the game stood at 3-2 after my second goal, a whirlwind of action, goals and fantastic drama with both sides having led.

We were touching the winning post in normal time when Lionel went wandering... from a corner, the ball came over and he tried to reach it when he was never ever going to get there because there were so many bodies piling in. Charlton's centre-back, a lad called Richard Rufus, who had never scored a goal in his career before, just nodded it back over Lionel's head and into the empty net. It was gutting. Five minutes to go or something.

I later heard Mark Bright say that he had seen that Perez was coming for the corner and so simply stood in front of him and made sure Lionel ran into him. We were back level again.

So we went into extra-time, and we should have sorted it out then too, but we didn't. We should have done. We worked a fantastic move for Nicky Summerbee to latch on to one of my laybacks and he buried it on the run from the edge of the area. A brilliant shot to make it 4-3. But then Mendonca scored a superbly athletic goal, leaping high to volley home a rebound to make the score an incredible 4-4.

Then it came to penalties. I had never taken one before in senior football, but I didn't feel bad about taking one, so they said I could go sixth if it went that far. So, of course, it went to 5-5 and now it was my turn. I absolutely never felt more confident in my life. Sasa Ilic was in goal for Charlton and I just remember eye-balling him, putting the ball down, and literally waiting for him to dive before I stroked it into the other corner. I felt fine. We'd all taken great penalties up to that point. Charlton took some very good penalties as well – neither keeper really got close to any of the first thirteen spot-kicks – but unfortunately for us Mickey [Gray] came up and perhaps he lacked the conviction. It didn't happen for Mickey. Ilic saved and went ballistic and we all felt the devastation and, of course, had to watch the Charlton boys on fire.

We had been so good in the second half of that season it was frightening. If the season had started at Christmas we'd have won the league by 15 points. We were fantastic. In the dressing room afterwards at Wembley we got together and said, "This is just a temporary set-back. We are the best team in this division by a mile. We're better than Charlton. We're better than the other two teams that went up ahead of us. We have to stay together, have a summer off and come back with everyone raring to go." It was a good strong message Bally gave out as I, Lee Clark and a couple of the other senior players did too.

And we did come back stronger. That game made us a better team – it galvanized us. And that next year we absolutely walked the division. We were head and shoulders above everybody. I'm not so sure that if we hadn't had that immense disappointment in the Play-offs, we would have been driven to bring the good years that followed.

Saying positive things after losing a play-off match is one thing, but often teams struggle the following year to get over the disappointment. But there was an understanding between us that we were the best team. We just had to keep the right attitude and make up for lost ground. We came back from the summer and had a fantastic year, one of the best years in football I've ever had.

The match in which we sealed promotion in 1998/99 was at Bury. I remember coming out and seeing three quarters of the ground full of our fans – away from home. That summed it up. It was a fantastic night. Just a lovely time. We went back to O'Neill's in Durham and stayed up most of the night.

It's true that after the match I smashed up the sign in our dressing room that proclaimed 'Nationwide League' and said a few things about how pleased I was to be out of it. The people from the Nationwide wrote to me, asking if it was the Nationwide Building Society itself I was angry with. I had to write back and apologize.

The secret of that team was that we worked hard together and played hard together. It was all or nothing. I'm trying to introduce that same kind of spirit now I'm back at Sunderland. I hope to make the players understand what it means to be a Sunderland player. I want them to share this dream with the people. They've got to stick their chests out and realize they are representing a region.

We did everything together. We socialized together – wives and girl-friends, families. We holidayed together, trained hard, won matches. We looked out for each other. We had a special bond that year and, of course, we found ourselves in the Premiership and that unity stuck. It eroded after three or four years – a few foreigners came in and the dressing room wasn't the same. [Allan] Johnston and [Nicky] Summerbee, who provided the ammunition for Kevin Phillips and myself weren't in the team anymore. Things slipped by. The thing had come to an end for me and I went back home to Ireland.

During the great years we had in the Premiership, two of the best days we had were the two 2-1 wins away to Newcastle. They were two great occa-sions. I remember the second one the most. A great friend of mine was there. He had come over from Ireland and wasn't a football man. He'd never been to a football match in his life and he was one of about 750 Sunderland fans they'd let in. He was being looked after by some of my friends from Seaham. It was a baptism of fire for him at his first match as he found himself in this cauldron, sitting there with Newcastle fans all around him. To start with he was scared stiff, but by the time he came out he was marching toward Newcastle Central station singing, "Sunderland 'til I die!" He was hooked.

He still talks about it. I was required for a urine sample and it took me ages to go, so the coach left without me. I left an hour or two later and went straight to the hotel at Seaburn, but the players had already left, so I didn't get to share the glory of that win with anyone in the team that night, so I went to Durham with my friend and our two wives. We were in a restaurant with the window open and all you could hear was people outside singing, "Sunderland 'til l die!" That was really good.

Before I came to Sunderland I'd played in London and Manchester, but it was different at Sunderland. It wasn't just a team doing well behind closed doors, and just peeping your head out to wave to the fans occasionally. We all did it and shared it together, we bought into the area as a team. We sold ourselves to the people, and they opened their hearts to us and let us in. We were a team and we knew at away games, that our crowd were going to lift us.

At home games it was superb. I remember playing Arsenal and I was standing in the tunnel before the match beside their Dutch winger Helder. We walked out of the tunnel to Prokofiev, the place was rocking and everywhere you looked there were red and white shirts. He said, "I thought they were for us," but I told him, "You're going to find out in a few minutes my friend!" We played them off the park, beat them and he never got a kick. That was what the crowd did for us in those days.

I could fast forward to just before I came back to the club. Things were going wrong. Players were scared – they didn't want to make mistakes and have everybody howling at them. My hope is to get those good days back.

Different clubs need different things. I think this club needs a connection between it and its fans. Sunderland needs passion, it needs heart, it needs commitment. It needs more than just professional football. Players at this club have got to live the dream. Eat, sleep and drink it. Share it. If we can get passion like that wearing the jersey we'll be fine.

I have to educate the players. I've got to make them understand what makes this club great, make them understand the efforts that the people who commit themselves to season tickets are making. Often they're working long shifts and overtime to get the money to come to support the club. I have to make sure players appreciate and never ever abuse that. I always had a desire to pay back the supporters. I want to create that here again. It might take me longer than people would like to create that, but it's vital. I have a group of players here we can get that from and a new manager in Roy Keane who will galvanise the place. I think it's vital to get that momentum rolling again, because I think the club only works when we have players from that mould who play for the team.

A great example of the people backing Sunderland was in my Benefit Match, when I played part of the game for Sunderland and part for Ireland. It was just a friendly, but to raise a million from that was unbelievable. It gave me huge pleasure to be able to split the money between charities in the city and over in Ireland.

This is the only club in the world I'd have got involved with in the way I have. It was at Cheltenham in March [2006] that things started to move. The week before that I spoke to a really astute businessman in London, who I knew would help me find a pathway to try and make a difference at club. I knew there was something there that wasn't being done right. I knew the people were disconnected with the team. I knew the whole thing was going the wrong way. But I knew nothing about how the business side of things was going. I was introduced to group of people in Cheltenham, who had been involved in the purchase of Manchester United. One guy said he'd look at it and he came back said, "go for it – put a team together."

To be truthful I had the idea in my head the day I left the club. John Fickling [Sunderland's former vice chairman] will admit that I said I would be back. He said, "I would love you to be manager at Sunderland." I told him that it maybe wouldn't be as manager, although I've been proved wrong there!

I actually left the club with the hump because I could clearly see what was happening, and I could see Bob [former chairman Bob Murray] making mistakes. My wife now calls what I'm doing, "unfinished business". Luckily I have really sporting people behind me, who love the idea that we might become a big club again. They're not in it for the money, this isn't like buying stock and shares to them. They're buying passion. They're passionate people. They already sponsor their teams in Ireland. I invited them to bring that to a place outside of Ireland.

I played many, many games in my career, but Sunderland is a really special place and as Chairman I want to show everyone how special it can be.

Subscribers

Name	Favourite Sunderland match	Competition, Year
Adamiok, Anthony	Newcastle United 2-1	League 1999
Alcock, Alan	Leeds United 1-0	FA Cup Final 1973
Alderson, Andrew	Charlton Athletic 4-4 (6-7pens)	Play-off Final 1998
Anderson, Bob	Manchester City 3-1	FA Cup Round 5 replay 1973
Anderson, John C	Manchester City 3-1	FA Cup Round 5 replay 1973
Anderson, Karl	Leeds United 1-0	FA Cup Final 1973
Arkle Green, Michael	Leeds United 1-0	FA Cup Final 1973
Askew, David	Manchester City 3-1	FA Cup Round 5 replay 1973
Attley, John George	Arsenal 2-1	FA Cup semi-final 1973
Averre, Steve	Chelsea 2-1	FA Cup Round 6 replay 1992
Bailey, Peter	Newcastle United 4-1	League 1979
Bailey, Victor Edward	Leeds United 1-0	FA Cup Final 1973
Bain, John	Wolves 0-0	League 1954
Bain, Steven	Chelsea 4-1	League 1999
Bainbridge, Ian	Chelsea 4-1	League 1999
Bainbridge, Keith	Liverpool 1-0	League 1981
Balmer, Mick	Manchester City 3-1	FA Cup Round 5 replay 1973
Barber, A G	West Ham 2-0	League 1980
Barber, Alan James	Manchester City 3-1	FA Cup Round 5 replay 1973
Barlow, David	Arsenal 2-1	FA Cup semi-final 1973
Barns, Stuart	Leeds United 1-0	FA Cup Final 1973
Barron, Andrew	Chelsea 4-1	League 1999
Barton, Ian	Liverpool 0-2	FA Cup Final 1992
Barton, Jillian	Chelsea 1-1	FA Cup Round 6 1992
Bates, Michael	Huddersfield Town 6-0	FA Cup 1950
Beadle Family	Chelsea 2-1	FA Cup Round 6 replay 1992

Bell, Joe	Leeds United 1-0	FA Cup Final 1973
Bell, Robbie	Sheffield United 2-0	Play-off semi-final 2nd leg 1998
Bell, Steve	Newcastle United 4-1	League 1979
Blacker, Anthony	Leeds United 1-0	FA Cup Final 1973
Blyth, Bill	Manchester United 3-3	FA Cup Round 6 1964
Booth, George	Charlton Athletic 2-1	League 1964
Brady, Kieran	West Ham 4-3	League 1989
Breeze, Lance Roger	Manchester United 3-2	League 1974
Brownless, Christine	Leeds United 1-0	FA Cup Final 1973
Burnip, Gordon	Leeds United 1-0	FA Cup Final 1973
Butler, John	Chelsea 2-1	FA Cup Round 6 replay 1992
Cadwallader, Martin	Sheffield United 6-1	League 1968
Cadwallader, Martin	Wolves 2-0	League 1969
Campbell, Anthony	Chelsea 4-1	League 1999
Campbell, Arthur	Chelsea 2-1	FA Cup Round 6 replay 1992
Campbell, Steven	Chelsea 4-1	League 1999
Campbell, Thomas	Chelsea 4-1	League 1999
Carne, Robert	Leeds United 1-0	FA Cup Final 1973
Carson, John	Liverpool 1-0	League 1981
Carton, Joseph	Charlton Athletic 4-4 (6-7pens)	Play-off Final 1998
Catchpole, Tony	Leeds United 1-0	FA Cup Final 1973
Chadwick, Nick	Chelsea 2-1	FA Cup Round 6 replay 1992
Chapman, Brian	WBA 6-1	League 1977
Chapman, Paul	Newcastle United 4-1	League 1979
Charlton, Jane	Arsenal 2-1	FA Cup semi-final 1973
Christie, Des	Newcastle United 2-0	Play-off semi-final 2nd leg 1990
Clark, Colin John	Newcastle United 2-0	Play-off semi-final 2nd leg 1990
Clark, Jack	Leeds United 1-0	FA Cup Final 1973
Clark, Jim	Leeds United 1-0	FA Cup Final 1973
Clark, John	Arsenal 2-	FA Cup semi-final 1973
Clark, Valerie J	Chelsea 4-1	League 1999
Cleary, Robert J	Leeds United 1-0	FA Cup Final 1973
Coates, Gary	Leeds United 1-0	FA Cup Final 1973

Cohen, Trevor	Manchester City 3-1	FA Cup Round 5 replay 1973
Coleman, Norman	Arsenal 2-1	FA Cup Round 3 1961
Coley, Bill	Wolves 2-0	League 1969
Collins, L C	Leeds United 1-0	FA Cup Final 1973
Collins, Wally	Charlton Athletic 4-4 (6-7pens)	Play-off Final 1998
Colman, Ben	Chelsea 2-1	FA Cup Round 6 replay 1992
Cook, Garry	Charlton Athletic 4-4 (6-7pens)	Play-off Final 1998
Cook, Kay	Manchester United 2-2	FA Cup Round 6 replay 1964
Cook, Thomas Ernest	Leeds United 1-0	FA Cup Final 1973
Copeland, Bill	Manchester City 3-1	FA Cup Round 5 replay 1973
Copeland, Ian	Arsenal 2-0	League 1996
Copeland, Peter	West Ham 2-1	League 2005
Craggs, Dr Tracy	Chelsea 3-2	League Cup semi-final 2nd leg 1985
Cresswell, David	Charlton Athletic 4-4 (6-7pens)	Play-off Final 1998
Crombie, David	Chelsea 4-1	League 1999
Crosby, Robert	Notts County 1-1	League 1978
Cummings, Chris	Newcastle United 2-1	League 2000
Currie, Dennis	Liverpool 1-0	League 1981
Dart, Colin	Manchester City 3-1	FA Cup Round 5 replay 1973
Davidson, Ian	Leeds United 1-0	FA Cup Final 1973
Davies, George	Leeds United 1-0	FA Cup Final 1973
Davis, Chris	Newcastle United 2-1	League 2000
Davis, Trevor	Charlton Athletic 4-4 (6-7pens)	Play-off Final 1998
Davison, John	Leeds United 1-0	FA Cup Final 1973
Davison, Laurie	Derby County 1-1	League 2003
Dawson, Keith	Charlton Athletic 4-4 (6-7pens)	Play-off Final 1998
Days, Harry (age 5)	Sunderland v Real Madrid 2010	
Dent, Anthony	Newcastle United 2-1	League 1999
Derivan, Tom	Newcastle United 2-0	Play-off semi-final 2nd leg 1990
Dimmock, Diane	Chelsea 4-1	League 1999
Dinning, Chris	Manchester United 3-3	FA Cup Round 6 1964

Dixon, Margaret Jane	Tottenham Hotspur 2-1	League Cup Round 4 replay 1984
Dobson, Mark	Charlton Athletic 4-4 (6-7pens)	Play-off Final 1998
Dobson, Paul sobs	Newcastle United 4-1	League 1979
Dodds, Jamie Eric	Newcastle United 2-1	League 2000
Douglas, Keith	Newcastle United 4-1	League 1979
Dunn, Jack	Manchester City 3-1	FA Cup Round 5 replay 1973
Eeles, Brian	Manchester City 3-1	FA Cup Round 5 replay 1973
Elliott, Graeme	Manchester United 2-2	FA Cup Round 6 replay 1964
Ellis, Dave	Newcastle United 2-1	League 2000
Ellis, Ted	Leeds United 1-0	FA Cup Final 1973
Ellison, Neil	Newcastle United 2-1	League 2000
Fairlamb, Paul	Newcastle United 4-1	League 1979
Fawell, Paul	Newcastle United 2-0	Play-off semi-final 2nd leg 1990
Felton, Peter	Leeds United 1-0	FA Cup Final 1973
Finn, Gerry	Leeds United 1-0	FA Cup Final 1973
Fitzgerald, Keith	Fulham 0-3	League 1966
Fleming, Shaun	Newcastle United 2-1	League 1999
Gambles, Ken	Leeds United 1-1	FA Cup Round 5 1967
George Courtley	Newcastle United 4-1	League 1979
Gibson, Michael P	Arsenal 2-1	FA Cup semi-final 1973
Gifford, Steve	Leeds United 1-0	FA Cup Final 1973
Gillis, Robert William	Arsenal 2-1	FA Cup semi-final 1973
Gilmore, Michael	Aston Villa 0-0	League 2000
Gilmore, Stephen	Newcastle United 2-0	Play-off semi-final 2nd leg 1990
Gold, Dominic S	Newcastle United 2-1	League 2000
Goodey, Thomas	West Ham 3-2	FA Cup Round 5 1992
Goodman, Michael	Newcastle United 4-1	League 1979
Graham, Davey	Newcastle United 2-1	League 2000
Green, Bob	Leeds United 1-0	FA Cup Final 1973
Guilbert, Tracey	Leeds United 1-0	FA Cup Final 1973
Hagan, Scott J	Manchester United 2-1	League 2003
Hall, Helen V	Oxford United 7-0	League 1998

Hall, Joseph	Manchester City 3-1	FA Cup Round 5 replay 1973
Hall, Mr	Crystal Palace 2-1	Play-off semi-final 2nd leg 2004
Halliday, Steven	Newcastle United 2-2	League 2000
Hallsworth, John	Tottenham Hotspur 1-1	FA Cup Round 6 1961
Hanson, Mark	Manchester City 3-1	FA Cup Round 5 replay 1973
Haram, Fred	Newcastle United 2-1	League 2000
Harding, Rob	Charlton Athletic 4-4 (6-7pens)	Play-off Final 1998
Hardman, David	Nottingham Forest 4-1	League 1996
Hardman, Jonathan	Bury 5-1	League 1999
Hardman, Paul	Manchester City 3-1	FA Cup Round 5 replay 1973
Harrison, Brian	Manchester City 3-1	FA Cup Round 5 replay 1973
Harrison, Brian Mark	Chelsea 2-1	FA Cup Round 6 replay 1992
Harrison, Robert	Manchester City 3-1	FA Cup Round 5 replay 1973
Haswell, Maureen	Newcastle United 4-1	League 1979
Haugh, Jack	Chelsea 2-1	FA Cup Round 6 replay 1992
Hazard, Jimmy	Birmingham City 2-0	FA Cup Round 5 replay 2004
Hays, Malcolm T	Leeds United 1-0	FA Cup Final 1973
Hebron, Neil	Leeds United 1-0	FA Cup Final 1973
Hendry, James William	Chelsea 4-1	League 1999
Heslop, David	Watford 0-8	League 1982
Hillam, Dave	Southampton 3-1	League 1961
Holder, Brian	Liverpool 2-0	FA Cup Round 4 1961
Holland, Daniel	Newcastle United 2-1	League 1999
Hopper, Stephen	Newcastle United 2-1	League 1999
Hossack, Robert	Leeds United 1-0	FA Cup Final 1973
Howells, Brian	Manchester City 3-1	FA Cup Round 5 replay 1973
Howells, Peter	Norwich City 1-0	FA Cup semi-final 1992
Hudson, Keith	Manchester City 3-1	FA Cup Round 5 replay 1973

Hunter, Andy	Leeds United 1-0	FA Cup Final 1973
Ingman, Richard	Chelsea 4-3	League 1955
Jackson, Les	Newcastle United 2-1	League 2000
Jackson, Tony	Manchester City 3-1	FA Cup Round 5 replay 1973
Jarrett, Marc Paul	Charlton Athletic 4-4 (6-7pens)	Play-off Final 1998
Johnson, Audrey	Stoke City 3-0	League 1998
Johnson, Tony	Newcastle United 2-0	Play-off semi-final 2nd leg 1990
Jon Stokoe	Tottenham Hotspur 2-1	League Cup Round 4 replay 1984
Keillor, Kevin	Chelsea 3-2	League Cup semi-final 2nd leg 1985
Kemp, Peter G	Manchester City 3-1	FA Cup Round 5 replay 1973
Kent, Jon	Chelsea 4-1	League 1999
Kidd, Gary	Newcastle United 4-1	League 1979
Kitchin, John	Manchester City 3-1	FA Cup Round 5 replay 1973
Lavelle, Michael	Newcastle United 2-0	Play-off semi-final 2nd leg 1990
Lawrence, Kevin	Leeds United 1-0	FA Cup Final 1973
Lawson, Steve	Newcastle United 2-0	Play-off semi-final 2nd leg 1990
Laydon, Jean	Newcastle United 2-1	League 1999
Lennox, Steve	West Ham 4-3	League 1990
Liddle, Alan	Charlton Athletic 4-4 (6-7pens)	Play-off Final 1998
Liddle, John	Chelsea 4-1	League 1999
Little, Thomas	Leeds United 1-0	FA Cup Final 1973
Love, Mike	Manchester City 3-1	FA Cup Round 5 replay 1973
Mabon, Gordon F	Charlton Athletic 4-4 (6-7pens)	Play-off Final 1998
Mackey, Colin	Leeds United 1-0	FA Cup Final 1973
Magee, Kevin	Leeds United 1-0	FA Cup Final 1973
Maith, John	Leeds United 1-0	FA Cup Final 1973
Mam's Debut	Blackburn Rovers 3-0	League 2001
Martin, Jim	Preston North End 3-3	FA Cup Round 4 1955
Mason Ian	Manchester United 2-2	FA Cup Round 3 replay 1996

Mason Philip	Chelsea 4-1	League 1999
Massingham, John	Chelsea 4-1	League 1999
Maughan, Richard	Chelsea 3-0	League 1996
McBurnie, Ian	Sheffield United 2-0	Play-off semi-final 2nd leg 1998
McCamley, John M	Leeds United 1-0	FA Cup Final 1973
McColl, Ryan	Manchester City 3-1	FA Cup Round 5 replay 1973
McCourt, Duncan	Chelsea 2-1	FA Cup Round 6 replay 1992
McIvor, Joe	Chelsea 2-1	FA Cup Round 6 replay 1992
McKenna, Harry	Leeds United 1-0	FA Cup Final 1973
Menham, Ian	Leeds United 1-0	FA Cup Final 1973
Middleton, Andrew	Charlton Athletic 4-4 (6-7pens)	Play-off Final 1998
Mills, Roy	Tottenham Hotspur 1-1	FA Cup Round 6 1961
Mitchinson, Ronald		
Moles, Darren	Chelsea 4-1	League 1999
Mooney, Stephen	Chelsea 2-1	FA Cup Round 6 replay 1992
Moran, Eric James	Chelsea 4-1	League 1999
Morgan, Peter	Swindon Town 1-0	Play-off Final 1990
Moscardini, Peter	Sheffield United 2-0	Play-off semi-final 2nd leg 1998
Murray, Paul	Newcastle United 4-1	League 1979
Murray, Sam	Chelsea 4-1	League 1999
Myers, John	Leeds United 1-0	FA Cup Final 1973
Neasham, Mick	Manchester City 3-1	FA Cup Round 5 replay 1973
Nelson, Bob	Nottingham Forest 3-0	League 1958
Nelson, David	Burnley 4-3	League 1971
Newman, Ted	Arsenal 2-1	FA Cup semi-final 1973
Newton, Brian		
Newton, Helen	Swindon Town 1-0	Play-off Final 1990
Nixon, Michael	Newcastle United 2-0	Play-off semi-final 2nd leg 1990
Nolan, Malcolm	Arsenal 7-1	League 1953
Otterburn, Ray	Newcastle United 1-4	League 2005

Patterson, Bryan	Manchester United 2-2	FA Cup Round 6 replay 1964
Patterson, Kevin	Chelsea 4-1	League 1999
Pedwell, Walter	Leeds United 1-0	FA Cup Final 1973
Peel, Tom	Charlton Athletic 4-4 (6-7pens)	Play-off Final 1998
Perez, Lionel	Stoke City 3-0	League 1998
Peterkin, Daniel	Watford 4-2	League 2005
Pickering, Douglas	Manchester City 3-1	FA Cup Round 5 replay 1973
Potter, Donald Brian	Leeds United 1-0	FA Cup Final 1973
Pratt, John Graham	Chelsea 2-1	FA Cup Round 6 replay 1992
Pyle, Brian	Charlton Athletic 4-4 (6-7pens)	Play-off Final 1998
Ralph, Alan	Newcastle United 3-0	League 1966
Ratton, Eamonn	Watford 4-2	League 2005
Ratton, Gerard Ciaran	Chelsea 3-2	League Cup semi-final 2nd leg 1985
Ratton, Tony	Newcastle United 2-0	Play-off semi-final 2nd leg 1990
Reed, Brian	Manchester United 3-2	League 1984
Richardson, Barrie	Manchester City 3-1	FA Cup Round 5 replay 1973
Ridley, Josh	Stoke City 1-0	League 2005
Ritchie, Marshall	Chelsea 2-1	FA Cup Round 6 replay 1992
Robertson Waite, William	Arsenal 2-1	FA Cup Round 3 1961
Robertson, Edward	Leeds United 1-0	FA Cup Final 1973
Rodgers, Dennis R	Leeds United 1-0	FA Cup Final 1973
Roger Mason,	Tottenham Hotspur 1-1	FA Cup Round 6 1961
Rooney, David	Chelsea 2-1	FA Cup Round 6 replay 1992
Rose, Alistair	Charlton Athletic 4-4 (6-7pens)	Play-off Final 1998
Royal, Glen	Newcastle United 2-0	Play-off semi-final 2nd leg 1990
Scarr, Mervyn	Leeds United 1-0	FA Cup Final 1973
Scott Derry	Tottenham Hotspur 2-1	League Cup Round 4 replay 1984
Scott, Pete	Everton 3-1	FA Cup Round 5 1964
Sheehan, Maurice	Charlton Athletic 4-4 (6-7pens)	Play-off Final 1998

Shepard, Leslie	Leeds United 1-0	FA Cup Final 1973
Short, Bob	Manchester United 3-3	FA Cup Round 6 1964
Simonnet, Anne	Manchester City 3-1	FA Cup Round 5 replay 1973
Simpson, Joe	Leeds United 1-0	FA Cup Final 1973
Sixsmith, Pete	Manchester City 3-1	FA Cup Round 5 replay 1973
Slater, David	Leeds United 1-0	FA Cup Final 1973
Smart, Frank	Charlton Athletic 4-4 (6-7pens)	Play-off Final 1998
Smith, David Stanley	Manchester City 3-1	FA Cup Round 5 replay 1973
Smith, Gordon L	Tottenham Hotspur 1-1	FA Cup Round 6 1961
Smith, Gregory G	Charlton Athletic 4-4 (6-7pens)	Play-off Final 1998
Smith, Leonard	Manchester City 3-1	FA Cup Round 5 replay 1973
Smithson, Andrew	Chelsea 3-0	League 1996
Spence, Alexander	Manchester United 2-2	League 1955
Spence, Craig	Newcastle United 2-0	Play-off semi-final 2nd leg 1990
Stephenson, Chris	Newcastle United 2-2	League 2000
Stephenson, Colin	Leeds United 1-0	FA Cup Final 1973
Stobbs, Terry	Leeds United 1-0	FA Cup Final 1973
Stoker, John	Leeds United 1-0	FA Cup Final 1973
Stokoe, James	Leeds United 1-0	FA Cup Final 1973
Stook, Desmond	Chelsea 2-1	FA Cup Round 6 replay 1992
Sweetlove, Kay	Manchester City 3-1	FA Cup Round 5 replay 1973
Taylor, David	Leeds United 1-0	FA Cup Final 1973
Taylor-Bard, Stuart	Charlton Athletic 4-4 (6-7pens)	Play-off Final 1998
Tennet, John	Manchester City 3-1	FA Cup Round 5 replay 1973
Thompson, Andrew	Newcastle United 2-1	League 2000
Thompson, Jim	Leeds United 1-0	FA Cup Final 1973
Thompson, Mark Lloyd	Sheffield United 2-0	Play-off semi-final 2nd leg 1998
Thompson, Nicholas	Charlton Athletic 4-4 (6-7pens)	Play-off Final 1998
Thompson, Peter	Manchester City 3-1	FA Cup Round 5 replay 1973

Thompson, Phillip	Chelsea 2-1	FA Cup Round 6 replay 1992
Tindall, Norman	Newcastle United 2-1	League 2000
Tivnen, Harry Dominic	Manchester City 3-1	FA Cup Round 5 replay 1973
Todd, Bob	Leeds United 1-0	FA Cup Final 1973
Todd, John	Leeds United 1-0	FA Cup Final 1973
Trotter, John Robert	Leeds United 1-0	FA Cup Final 1973
Turley, Alan	Manchester City 3-1	FA Cup Round 5 replay 1973
Unsworth, Jonathan	Newcastle United 2-1	League 2000
Urwin, Jack	Newcastle United 2-2	League 1958
Usher, David	Newcastle United 2-1	League 1999
Waddleton, Peter	Newcastle United 4-1	League 1979
Walker, Brian	Leeds United 1-0	FA Cup Final 1973
Walker, Matthew Joseph	Rotherham United 1-0	League 2005
Walsh, Arthur	Leeds United 1-0	FA Cup Final 1973
Walton, James	Millwall 6-0	League 1995
Walton, Paul	Newcastle United 2-1	League 1999
Walton, Ron	Manchester City 3-1	FA Cup Round 5 replay 1973
Warriner, John	Arsenal 2-1	FA Cup Round 3 1961
Watson, Derek	Arsenal 2-1	FA Cup Round 3 1961
Watt, John C	Leeds United 1-0	FA Cup Final 1973
Watt, John Gilstin	Manchester United 3-3	FA Cup Round 6 1964
Wells, Trevor	Charlton Athletic 4-4 (6-7pens)	Play-off Final 1998
Wilding, Dave	Newcastle United 1-0	League 1980
Wilkinson, Paul	Chelsea 3-0	League 1996
Williams, Denis	West Brom 6-1	League 1977
Wilson, Andrew Robert	Newcastle United 2-1	League 1999
Wood, John Richard	Leeds United 1-0	FA Cup Final 1973
Young, Colin	Charlton Athletic 4-4 (6-7pens)	Play-off Final 1998
Young, Darren	Chelsea 4-1	League 1999
Young, Mark	Derby County 2-1	League 2006

Top Seven Games Voted For		No. of Votes
Leeds United 1-0	FA Cup Final 1973	60
Manchester City 3-1	FA Cup Round 5 replay 1973	35
Charlton Athletic 4-4 (6-7 pens)	Play-off Final 1998	23
Chelsea 4-1	League 1999	19
Chelsea 2-1	FA Cup Round 6 replay 1992	16
Newcastle United 2-0	Play-off semi-final 2nd leg 1990	12
Newcastle United 4-1	League 1979	12